Accessing Our Humanity
Omar Bitar

Published by FlowerPublish
© Omar Bitar 2021
ISBN 978-1-989352-38-0

FlowerPublish
www.flowerpublish.com
Montreal, Canada

Table of Contents

Simpler is Better..5
In The Moment..13
Misconceptions...30
Normal is Not Always Normal............................42
Social Media and Technology............................57
The Blind Spot..68
It's More Fun to Be Happy.................................87
Right, Logic and Valid.......................................98

Simpler is Better

The pursuit of happiness and indulgence in self-comfort has become a trend when it should simply be something natural. We spend too much time talking about wanting to be happy and desperately try to be comfortable with ourselves instead of realizing such things are easily achieved with the right way of thinking. Everything in our lives begins with us, we forget how much control we actually have for what takes place in our minds. It is true, comfort in yourself is the solution to life's problems. And it's logical; your thoughts and feelings come from you, they may be influenced from the outside environment but why should that mean it overpowers our control over the way we think?

"Life is not black and white, it's grey." A common phrase that is used to describe how the world is not divided into dark and light, that there is a mixture of both. We cannot categorize good and bad, we all have both inside of us. Most of us have been through enough situations that, to some extent, we react better every time, or that we are improving in certain areas. Each day we work in order to reach our maximum potential.

The term potential is often misinterpreted as our maximum ability. The truth is, there is no top level we'll reach and achieve, we keep improving – if we do things right – till the day we die. This is all common and cliché knowledge; everyday we do things that make us grow and develop into better people. But what does that really mean?

I would rephrase it to "Life *is* black and white, *and people* are grey". We are shaped from our experiences that are either good or bad, and that's what characterizes our personalities. But just because a situation is considered to be bad, why does that mean no good can come from it? The state of a situation should have no influence with the way we think.

We all know enough to realize that no one is purely good, the same way no one is purely bad – unless of course we refer to Zionists. The common idea is to understand that we are capable of doing both good and bad, and that our actions are what matters.

The outcomes of all affairs are determined. If something is meant to go elsewhere it will never come to you. And if something is yours by destiny, nothing will stand in your way to receive it. There's comfort in knowing that our path is set. We just have to do what we believe to be right and hope for the best. Time goes faster when we're having fun. Life is fun when things are good. I don't see a reason for things to not *be* good when we control the perspective we have over situations.

Experiences are basically training. Some sessions are harder than others and some sessions are worse, but that does not mean we don't benefit from them. It's the exact opposite actually; there is always more good in bad situations than in the good ones, and when we learn to see them in every situation we face we reach the solution. We learn best from our experiences; the things we go through impact our way of thinking and the way we feel about certain situations.

It is important to care about what others think. If you don't then you should surround yourself with better people. Our world is all about connectedness. We think it's about individuality but at the end of the day we're all linked through our experiences and our actions. An ideal world is when everyone's opinion matters, and we respect the way people think. I feel people gave up on the idea of solidarity because they believe there is no point.

"The end of the world is inevitable but hopefully it's still a long way from coming."

This world may be far from perfect but it's really not that bad, so let's stop with this dark bullshit and make a change for the good of our lives.

Our relationships with people mean nothing if we don't have a good relationship with ourselves. If you own a business and employ thousands of people you are responsible for each of them. If something goes wrong, even though you took every precaution necessary, it's still your fault. Because when you're in charge, you're responsible for what happens. It's the same when it comes to your way of thinking. No one can control what we do. People can trigger certain attributes that push us to do certain things, but the choices come from us. Just like how a business has many employees, our way of thinking has a lot of different perspectives that are influenced by logic and emotion. We may not have control over the obstacles we face on the inside, but we have control over what we choose to portray on the outside. And since we have a lot of perspectives, we should learn to figure out which are the best ones when it comes to dealing with our problems.

When you run your business you want the best employees working, not the reckless ones. If those are the insurances that we give our work we should do the same for ourselves. We're all stronger than we think we are. Unfortunately, we live in a world that has a bit of a shitty vibe when it comes to mental stability. There are so many different diagnoses and scientific labels that make us forget the simplicity of our minds. Most of the time the simplest way is the best way, that's why it's the simplest way. There are already so many complicated things in this world, and as the years go by things that should be simple are getting more and more complex. So many of these things we can't control, or at least it's difficult to find a way to interfere. But something that we can control is our way of thinking. We choose to limit the ability of our minds due to the distractions around us.

By the end of this book I'm hoping you understand how simple thinking really is, and how much smarter you get when you take the path of simplicity. It's like that quote we find on stupid memes; don't think hard, think smart. Our brain is our engine, let's not fuck up the engine. The world's atmosphere sometimes leads us to believe that everything in life is complicated and nothing is as simple as it sounds. It's your brain. If you choose that you want to think logically then your logic is what you will find. And when has thinking logically ever been the wrong choice?

What exactly is knowledge though? It's what we know, but how do we know if it's right? Imagine you're sitting at home watching TV. It's late at night, the windows are closed and you have the volume of the TV pretty loud. You hear a sound of thunder and you tell yourself that it's raining outside. The sound came from the TV show you're watching, but you think it's from outside. However, it actually is raining outside. You came to that conclusion – the right conclusion – based on something that wasn't true, because the thunder came from the TV. Is that actual knowledge that you know it's raining outside?

When we're told to think in certain ways about certain issues, we do them because it makes sense. We came to the right conclusion but with the wrong method. The things we do are not supposed to be done just because we think it's true, we actually have to believe it. Life isn't about living in the moment like we're led to believe. It's about considering our past by learning from our mistakes and making the right choices in the present, so we're put in a better position in the future. That is the reason for past, present and future. To keep track of ourselves and what we do. Everything that happened was meant to happen. We can never change it, so instead we choose to accept it. No one can go back in time and change the things they've done.

There's no such thing as time travel, time is just an illusion that is there for us to not be late for work or know what time to go to sleep. Even though the idea of time travel has given us amazing entertainment like the shows Dark and Lost, time is just a universal method to know when we should do the things we want to do each day.

With that we know that we each have our own timeline. Everyone is on track on their own path. The worst thing to do is to compare our life with others, because we're each on the task we're supposed to be on. Especially when we're facing troubled times. We must always remember that every single situation we face has some kind of benefit. It doesn't matter if most of your friends graduated and you're still studying, it doesn't matter if they're getting married and you're still single, all that matters is that you're doing whatever it is you're supposed to be doing. Everything comes in its own time. When we accept that, not only are we happier in our current positions, but we don't waste any of the time that passes dwelling on something pointless.

The grass is always greener on the other side, and that's because of perception. We think that something is better when it's just different. Everything has advantages and disadvantages, and disadvantages should be seen as a key to a greater advantage. Life is only as bad as we make it out to be. We need to stop this trend of negativity and understand why we're all here; to live and learn.

Realize something; things aren't meant to be bad. When things seem bad it's only there for us to learn as one of life's tests. It's like when we tell someone we care about that they're doing something wrong. We're not saying it to hurt their feelings, we say it for their benefit. Whether it hurts their feelings or not is their choice, as long as they see how it benefits them at the end of the day. With that example we see that there is no point for it to hurt us, and see where the people who care about us are coming from. Life isn't trying to hurt us; it just puts us in certain situations for us to improve and be grateful for everything. When we remember that, we find it a lot easier to enjoy every moment whether good or bad, and find ourselves dealing with life more comfortably.

We're all visual learners. That's why mistakes are regarded as the things that shape who we are, and as the lessons we learn in life. It's logic; when we see how we went wrong and what we faced as a consequence we learn not to do it again. We're all capable of thinking about what could very well turn out to be a mistake. But when we actually do them we don't just see, we feel. Emotions are an extremely important part when it comes to who we are, as it speaks for the heart. Everyone should listen to their heart, because those who cannot trust their heart are lost.

We can always grow up a little more. The idea of growing up is not about age. From the ages of sixteen to twenty I was still acting like I was ten. It's also not about the experiences we face, it's how we deal with them and come out the other side. It's easy to just go on cruise control and wait for the situation to be over. That's the way we let life pass us by. But when we take every situation as a challenge to better ourselves, we access our humanity.

The trick is to love yourself. If there's one person who won't betray you and will always know what's best for you it's yourself. You'll find it difficult to like people if you can't like yourself. We should always remember to be confident. Confidence isn't about believing that you're the best and that people will love you, it's about knowing you *do* your best and you're fine whether people love you or not.

The fact is you have to pick a side; either have situations control your way of thinking or have your way of thinking control the situation. It's really that simple, take the time to think and you'll see there's always a solution to everything. Things get hard but we're always rewarded for it afterwards.

The loser of today is the winner of tomorrow. In this case, if you choose to accept the suffering and feel the pain you will only find success in the aftermath. I like to think of my life as a large staircase that I keep climbing everyday. The stepping stones are either dark or light, depending on what I've experienced. Either way, both types always move me up. It's nice to look back and see how far we've come, remember the days of darkness and where it led us.

When we see that everything we face brings us up even though it feels like it's pushing us down we come to terms with the fact that everything is really for our benefit. Like we said, life doesn't hate us, it just wants to teach us.

It's like exercising for example; we train to look better and eventually it makes us feel good, comfortable in our physicality. The more time and work we put in the more improvements we see. It's the exact same thing when it comes to our minds. The more we think logically the more we understand that life is our friend who can sometimes be tough; we strengthen the way we think, and the way we see the world brightens. The idea of dominant positivity is always linked to fantasy lands or something that is just an illusion. But who said we can't make fantasy a reality? I see nothing wrong with benefitting from everything that happens around me. I would much rather make the bad situations my bitch rather than me a slave to them.

      The whole point of the book you're about to read is for you to realize that things don't have to be the way they seem, nor the way they are. We can all agree this world isn't exactly perfect. We can also agree that there have been so many times we let life beat us down and make us feel like shit. We try to find the solution in inspirational posts, quotes on happiness, or in trying to convince ourselves things are not that bad. The best realization you'll make is that you'll find all your answers in front of you, you just need to know where to look and how to see it.

In The Moment

Life is like a Mario Game. This is a very interesting philosophy one of my mother's friends once told me. If you ever played the original Mario games you would know each level involves you running, jumping, smashing your head on blocks, sinking through tunnels, and fighting through obstacles. It's the same with us; we feel things are moving too fast and we can't keep up, we're finding ourselves in positions that we don't know how we reached, we feel the pain of the things we're going through, we feel like we're hitting rock bottom, or we face certain difficulties that require our time and effort. Just like life, the level seems stressful and you begin to feel frustrated.

At the end of the level, when you finally reach the finish line you feel a lot of relief and satisfaction. You pride yourself for finishing it. When you go on to the next level, everything repeats. The running, the jumping, the tunnels, even the fucking turtles. Each level is always the same, we are always doing the same shit and facing obstacles. We get the same feelings of frustration, the same thoughts of giving up, but when we realize that we're getting closer to Bowser we keep going.

So whenever we ask ourselves why we continue to have problems in our life, we'll remember the Mario Philosophy; when things are getting bad again, we should consider the fact that we're above the person we used to be. We're always going to be facing problems, and we're always going to get that feeling of frustration. When we ask ourselves why this is happening again, remember you're a level above where you were. It's all about the way you see it.

Many years ago I was given the best advice anyone can give me, and it took me a very long time to truly understand what it meant. I hope by the end of this book you will understand it much sooner than I did; if you don't like something change it, and if you can't change it then change the way you think about it.

Gandalf the Grey told us something similar; all of us who see dark times wish it never came to us, but we cannot decide what comes to us. All we have to decide is what to do with the given situation.

Life is not a test; it is full of them. The desire to want positive experiences is itself a negative experience, and the acceptance of negative experiences is a positive experience. Wanting to be happy and waiting for things to be different is counterproductive. We have all been told multiple times that the first step to solving a problem is accepting it. It's not just accepting the issue that is needed to be done, the importance is the way we react to it; whether we have to do something or find a perspective where we gain something.

There were many times when we let our experiences control the way we feel. Too many of us have been impacted by our environments when it comes to the way we think. We cannot change reality and the events that take place around us, but we can change the way we think and feel about it. Our brain is one of the very few things in this world that solely belongs to us. Why should we allow anyone but ourselves to control the way it works?

Feelings, thoughts, and actions come from within. We feel certain things, think about what we should do, then go ahead and do it. It all comes from the inside. Since that's the case, we should always remember that no matter what, our state of mind is controlled by us, and only us. With that in mind, it's all about perspective and logic, and if we see things clearly we find the logic.

Most of us are familiar with the fight or flight theory. The theory explains that when faced against a predator, our human instinct is to either attack the threat directly or run away from it. Obviously, if an animal comes at you, you're either going to attack it or run. We're not going to sit and reason with it. But we're not animals. Our thoughts aren't animals, and neither are our feelings. We have the time to decide what to do with the situation we're in. The fight or flight theory is a physiological response, but I believe that there is a psychological correlation when it comes to the way we deal with our situations.

We face a lot of problems everyday, the world itself already has its issues on top of our personal ones. There are already so many things that we cannot control, why not master the one thing that we can have full control of; the way we think. Something I wonder is that just because we face certain negative experiences in our lives, why does that mean our feelings towards them should be negative as well?

We make our best decisions when we're happy, feeling some sense of power, and when we feel in control. The point in the advice given to me all those years ago was that since there are so many situations we cannot control, we can always control the way we think about them. When we have control over our way of thinking and allow ourselves to have a logical view by eliminating the impact of the environment, we have the power to decide the way we act. With that power we make the right choices, choices that we made ourselves and without the influence of external negativity, and in my opinion that is the meaning of happiness.

Things go on either way, if we are put in situations we cannot change our best option is to see it in a way that has a benefit, otherwise we miss an opportunity at self-growth.

We always have a better view of things from above. If you stand on a cliff you can either look out into the horizon or look over an entire city. From your balcony you can see your whole garden. And when we think of the situation we're in with a mindset above it all we see things more clearly. When we're told to ask ourselves if something is itself right, that does not mean repeat it in our mind and come to the same conclusion. If we don't alter our perspective to a higher position, then we miss the point entirely.

When we're feeling down and find it difficult to think clearly, we sometimes find ourselves asking other people for help. There is nothing wrong with that at all. Those of us who are lucky enough to have people around us to help should take advantage of that. But I personally would rather find that mindset inside of me that I can go to whenever I want. That above perspective that we can find in ourselves that will always be there to aid us.

We all have multiple perspectives that are there. I believe that situations aren't what cause us to do certain things, they just bring to light the part of us inside that would. When we feel sad, it could trigger insecurities that influence the way we think and act. When a situation makes us angry, it triggers rage and we act irrational. We also find ourselves sometimes bottling up the emotions, and trying to run away from it. This is the fight or flight theory correlation I was talking about. When things get sad, we either feel sad or avoid it. My point is a middle ground, where we choose the way we think about the situations we cannot control, based on our neutral mindset to reach a logical solution. To do that, we have to know ourselves and how we work, so that we learn how to be in control. The best way to get to know people is talking to them.

Communication itself is one of the most important things in our world today. Before learning how to communicate with other people we must know how to communicate with ourselves. Who better to communicate with than a person who you know everything about. There's nothing wrong with talking to yourself. But when you talk to yourself you should talk to the part of yourself you trust to help you in the given situation, and you find that within you when you truly take a step back and lay everything out in front of you with a neutral mindset. We're capable of doing it because we've seen ourselves think logically in many different situations. Since we can do it in those circumstances, why can't we do it when we need it the most? Control, power, happiness. You really think you can't control the way you think? If we can't then who can? Are you going to wash your car in the rain? Are you going to deal with sadness by listening to sad music? When things are shit you don't take another shit on top of it; you get a shovel and clean it. That shovel comes from you.

Remember that asking yourself is not simply retelling yourself the situation. When you ask yourself, you ask that part of yourself that thinks from above. You take a step back to alter your mind into that perspective, and you think of a solution from there. I know it all sounds confusing, but once you realize you can build an outlook within yourself that you can trust, you'll realize you don't need anyone's help when it comes to your problems. That part of you just gets stronger and stronger with every situation you face. And when we learn to respond best to self-criticism, no one can control the way we feel. Build that part of you inside that tells you when you're being an idiot, tells you when you're doing something wrong.

Think about it this way. Psychologists and Psychiatrists have devoted their lives into understanding the way the human mind works. They have the ability to help people with their problems and guide them in the right direction. The information they need in order to do this comes from the patients themselves. They won't know how to help without it. Yes, certain people face extremely difficult mental obstacles that require the assistance of a professional, but most of us have strong minds that enable us to deal with our own issues. The point I am making is that all we have to do is let things unfold; minimize the complications, structure our minds to the above position we want it to be in, and we can find our own solutions. Have a mindset that is your own psychologist, you don't have to have a PhD to understand logic. It really doesn't take a genius to think.

Our brain is a muscle, the more we train it the more it can do. At the beginning we're going to find difficulties when it comes to thinking this way in tough situations. When we learn to process properly in every situation it becomes natural. The more we think the smarter we'll be. Think properly and simply, you'll be so much happier, and life will be a lot easier.

By the way, this is not my idea of wisdom, it's logic. I really don't see myself as a wise person; wisdom comes with time and I'm only twenty-two. I just feel like this is a smart way of thinking as it helped me through my own problems. But forget about the idea of wisdom, because being wise is simply living logically without the need to show it or think too much about it. Think logically and you'll be comfortable with yourself to the point where you don't feel the need to prove something, and you just live and be happy. You might argue that some problems cannot be solved easily. Don't misunderstand, I'm not saying any of this is easy, but it gets easier eventually, and it's definitely better than allowing situations to control the way we think. We put effort into a lot of things in our lives, and many of those things are pointless. Let's put in the effort when it comes to mental stability, because with that everything else will come naturally.

Something my mother drilled into my brain a very long time ago is that everything happens for a reason. I always believed it, and things would happen where I would actually see that it's true. Eventually we all need to realize that everything *does* happen for a reason. I say realize because we shouldn't pretend and just tell ourselves things to make us feel better. That's reality; there is a benefit to everything we face, even if we don't see it at the moment. This is one of the good things in life. There are already so many bad things, so let's just believe the good things and not try to convince ourselves our world is as dark as it seems, because it's really not.

Life goes on regardless. Problems are going to happen, so take advantage of them. I like to see problems as slingshots. They are obstacles that pull us backwards, but once dealt with we shoot further than where we were before. We don't want to be put back in the same mindset we were at before, what was the point of the problem then? Get pulled back, accept it, deal with it so when it's done you move two levels up. Considering the stepping stone philosophy that I mentioned earlier; every dark stepping stone is followed by two light ones. Take advantage of the situation and avoid letting it take advantage of you.

None of us are supposed to change; we're supposed to evolve. I have made many mistakes that I wish I could take back, but with that I realized that since we can't take them back we can use them to our benefit when we base who we want to go on to be. They're there and they're not going anywhere. Use them to your advantage. Many of the mistakes we make we learn from them in the moment, but many others take time, and we learn from them when we look back. We shouldn't aim to change. Everything we did, no matter how big the mistake, is a part of who we are. When we own it and use it to our advantage it becomes a strength rather than a weakness.

I want to make it clear that I have absolutely no idea what you're going through. I don't know the hardships you have gone through in life, I don't know the things you had to endure, and I definitely don't know the things you have done to get to the point you are in now. All I know is that there is a solution for everything, and when we learn to accept that everything happens for a reason there is nothing we should stress about. I also know that the way we think has a major influence on our happiness, and we're all capable of doing it. If we start from ourselves, fix our own problems first, we'll be able to be fit for others. It's not selfish to work on yourself, it's the complete opposite. Imagine a life where we're comfortable with ourselves. Be comfortable with yourself, hopefully we'll all get there with the proper way of thinking.

When we remember our past issues we realize that things were better than they seemed backed then. When we look at other people's problems, or at the drama characters face in the TV series we watch, we see the solutions to their problems and how they're overreacting. That is because we are in a neutral mindset. We are not influenced by the situation itself. Why can't we use that mindset when it comes to our personal problems, since it's there. We always complain how we can help others better than we help ourselves. It's like doing someone else's assignment, we always feel like we did better than we normally do for our own. That is because we eliminate the stress part of the assignment, and we just do it. It's the same case when we come to our problems; eliminate the stress of the environment.

There's nothing wrong with taking the time to think about the situation at hand. Most of the situations we face today are not seconds away from death; we always have time to take that step back. The things we rush we end up regretting, you'll never go wrong with thinking before acting. Just relax and think.

Something we fail to do in such an operating world is take that step back to see the bigger picture. It's difficult with everything that takes place in our everyday lives. But doing it only prevents current problems from escalating and further problems from happening. It's hard to do when facing troubled times as our nature is to either face it head on or run away from it, again, the fight or flight theory.

Running away makes us blinded from the situation as a whole and an answer will never be reached. And although facing the problem directly with full force often solves our problems, following our instinct is not always the right decision.

I believe that our instinct is not our body telling us what is right, but showing us what is deep down. That isn't always the right choice. Sometimes we think about things, and the conclusion we come to could be wrong. That is when our emotions come to help us make the right decisions. With instinct, it's purely what we want to do with eliminating the emotional and logical perspectives we have, and that should not always be counted on.

We all have emotions. We all feel something; some more than others. We either channel them into specific ones, or we feel and emphasize all our emotions in certain scenarios. We all like to believe we can control them. We can't. What we can control is how we react towards them, and which ones we choose to influence the way we think and take action. It isn't cool to not have emotions; it's completely senseless. Instead of fighting what is inside us we should use it. It's funny how hard people try to fight their emotions when it's what your heart is telling you. Our mind shows logic and our heart shows emotion. We have both so let's use both. We can't control what we feel, but we can choose what we want to do. Think of them as your advisors.

It's okay for certain things to be on our mind, what we should avoid is to have it control us. You're not a bad person for thinking bad things. Otherwise we're all bad people.

Sirius Black once said that the world isn't divided into good and bad people, we all have light and dark inside of us. What matters is the path we choose to take. You're a good person, I'm a good person, we're all good people, most of us at least. If you take the time to read a book that is under the self-help genre then I'm pretty sure you're a good person, I don't think psychopaths or Israelis would read this.

There is a reason we have both a heart and a mind. How we feel and how we should think must go hand in hand. We cannot be blamed for what we feel. When we see that we are capable of making decisions with both our hearts and minds we truly understand what it means to access our humanity.

They're literally the two most important parts of our body, if we can't trust them then what exactly do we trust in ourselves? Our ass? The true test lies in the decisions we make when acting upon a certain feeling. We all know this. Yet we find ways to be consumed in our emotions or disregard it entirely. We're not animals, our ability to think logically and reasonably are what differentiate us from them.

      We spend too much time prolonging our feelings of despair and digging ourselves deeper into it leaving us with nothing but more problems. If we learn to trigger that part of us where we think logically and reasonably whenever we feel certain negative emotions, we learn to overcome problems faster. Most of the times I felt angry – and there were a lot of times – I made mistakes that I regret. Thankfully, I was angry enough times to be able to remember the pain I felt in that regret. That's when I realized what it meant when Mr. Dunbar told me that only an idiot makes a mistake twice; when we actually learn from them there's no way we do it again with a clear mind, we do it again when we don't think, and who doesn't think? An idiot. Mr. Dunbar made me feel like I was an idiot every time I touched something hot knowing it's going to burn. But that's not what he meant. That genius of a man meant something much deeper than my thirteen-year-old mind could ever understand; in the moment we just have to remember all those times we were angry and where it led, and remember all those times we were calm and where it led. you'll find your answer in being calm, unless you're an idiot. Thank you Mr. Dunbar.

      We all like to complain that life is not fair. It is fair. Fair is not the same as convenient. A lot of bad things have happened in my life and I know I deserved them. I know I have made mistakes and that

I was punished for them. We all have been. The same way we were rewarded when we did good. We all deserve what we get. One of the things to accept when we face a problem is that it is happening for a reason. Whether this is karma and we have done something to deserve it, or this is one of life's major tests that shapes our personality. We have to be realistic, and it's really not that bad. I would rather have to face reality with every problem I have and acknowledge the reason for all of it rather than be ignorant and benefit from nothing. It's realistic to think everything has a benefit, and it's very logical. I don't believe that things just happen for nothing, and neither should you. What the hell is the point then?

Sometimes we just have to accept that we're assholes and we deserve it. We even come closer to a solution when we realize that.

Things will happen. Time goes on. We need to always remember what Gandalf told Frodo that day in the shire, and what Ksenia told me all those years ago; there are things we cannot change, and for us to benefit from them we need to see things differently, see things more clearly from above. Let's not ask why, and just say okay to the situation that comes. Work with ourselves to find a solution. Accepting it leads to solving it, and solving it properly leads to not repeating it.

We've heard the phrase 'play with the hand you're dealt' many times before. Those of us who play poker know that sometimes we need to fold because our hand is absolute shit. But with life it's different. You can't magically give yourself a Royal Flush on a poker table in a casino by just believing. There's nothing you can physically do for that to happen.

Luckily, life isn't a poker table, and we don't just have two options when it comes to our choices.

We have infinite possibilities. And the hand each of us are dealt has a lot of potential. No one has it better than others; just different. Take advantage of what you have, use it to your benefit rather than try to look for something that isn't yours. When we learn to be happy with what we have we no longer feel the urge to want more. That is when we're comfortable with ourselves.

We go through different periods in our lives; we face good times and bad times. Step by step we work through problems and the time goes on. Like we said, when we can't change something we view it in a better way. But we also face things that we *can* change.

We've all procrastinated. Whether it was a project or something we had to do. Every day we just keep pushing it further. That's because everyday we're in the exact same position we were at the time we chose to procrastinate, so what makes us think it's going to be different? When we start it today, then continue a little bit more the next, and keep increasing every day, we finish what we needed to do, because everyday we're a step closer to completion. It's the same with thinking; if we put the effort everyday to push ourselves to act on our rational thoughts with time it will become natural. That's the whole point; for this way of thinking to become natural. If you don't want it that's fine, please understand that I am not saying this is the best or smartest way, but it is a way. A way for us to make our own choices and live a life controlled by us.

No one can disagree that one of the master keys to happiness is patience. The thing about patience is that no matter how much we think we have it; it always manages to run thin in different circumstances. None of us are either patient or impatient, we're patient at times and impatient at others. Patience is a period, and its length depends on our view of the current situation. So you're either more, or less. You can be patient when you're holding your hunger, but impatient when it comes to listening to someone's extremely long story. It's all dependent on the situation, and it's just a period we need to get through, because everything passes.

It's important that we see our tasks as something we benefit from, and not something we have to do. It feels like our troubles are never ending when we let them take advantage of us, and with that lack of control we begin to lose patience. When we see how we can take advantage of it and use it, things become more interesting. Our problems go by much faster when we use things to our benefit rather than avoid them. It's fun to be happy, and frustrating to not be. Have fun, time goes by faster and life is a lot better.

There's no way I can go on a diet. If I wake up telling myself I want to go on a diet, by 4pm I would have eaten the entire house. Especially when I got extremely fat during the start of the pandemic, when everyone had to isolate and sit on their asses. But when I thought of it as sacrificing at least one month of my life with torture so that I can lose weight again I realized something; it's just a period. Get through it right and you won't have to face it again. I drank a fruit smoothie every morning, I absolutely hate fruits and held my vomit every time. I did that so after this period I won't have to drink another one of those things ever again. I decided to exercise like crazy everyday so when I reach my goal I can chill a bit with the intensity. I also cut off one of the best things in our world when I stopped eating sour patch. I did that so that when I reach my goal I can enjoy life without the feeling of having something to do. The point of all this is not to tell you I gained a lot of weight and lost it, it's to show that sometimes we shouldn't just live in the moment. Sometimes we are put in positions where we need to actually do something and think of the future. We only change the way we think of things when we can't change what's happening, it's important to know the difference.

Every moment we should ask ourselves if this is who we want to be, and at times we need to do something. I don't know you, I don't know the problems you have. All I know is that patience is just a period. And when we see the benefit in that period and where it can lead us it's easier to *be* patient. Some problems require more time and effort than others, we should allow it to happen. The further we're pulled back when we're on the slingshot, the further we'll be shot forward once relieved from our task. Let the reward fuel your motivation. So know what the reward is so you never lose sight of what you're fighting towards.

To truly understand our own way of thinking in the moments we're in is to know how our brain works. We do that by recollecting. There is a trend in this world where we shouldn't have regrets. I believe we should have regrets; they help us remember the severity of mistakes and where it can lead us. We should not grieve over what has passed unless it makes us work harder for what is about to come. We need to choose our regrets more logically, choose to remember the ones that remind us to stay on track.

When put in the moment there is always time to take a step back. Sometimes not saying anything is best, and gives us a chance to think. I never regretted my silence, but I regretted the things I've said many times.

I find that sometimes we forget what we've been through, and with that we can forget who we are. No one has it better than others, everyone lives different lives and we need to learn to take full advantage of our own. It's a lot better to remember and see who we really are than try to think about who we're not. Most of the time we're happier that way, and if not at least we know we need to make some changes. Keep up with yourself, keep checking in because no one else can do it better than you can.

A piece of metal becomes an axe after it gets hit blow by blow, and beaten up endlessly. The more we go through the stronger we get; we all know this. Don't just accept the problem, make it your bitch. If we're not going to own it then it's going to own us.

Something that helps when it comes to dealing with your issues is to see the advantage that can come with it. When we have a goal, achieving it can come with bonuses. Those bonuses could be seen as small, petty or insignificant to be the reason for our efforts. So I like to use these things as fuel to my ambition. These reasons sometimes motivate us more than the bigger picture. The bonuses we receive are important to us, just because it's wrong for it to be the reason for our motivation doesn't mean it can't help push us forward a little bit.

We should learn to remember and embrace regret. Regret is a painful feeling, and is sometimes one of the best wake-up calls. Many of our regrets make us feel uncomfortable. It's in there and it's not going anywhere. Again; if you can't change it then change the way you think about it. Make your regrets lessons for your future self instead of shame for your past self. Wouldn't you rather make it something positive for the times to come rather than make it negative for the times that passed?

It's not just about how we see things in the moment, it's about how we see the bigger picture. Everything around us is there for us to consume and better ourselves, all of us have different experiences. It's important to see how things really are. We're all unique so let's take advantage of that by accessing our humanity.

Misconceptions

We have all heard or read about the prisoners' dilemma from so many different sources, and every single one of them explains it as though they were the first people to identify this theory. I'm going to do the same.

Two members of a gang of robbers have been arrested; Tronte and Torben. The police are interrogating them in separate rooms and can only prove the case against them if they manage to have at least one of them testify. If they both choose to stay silent, then they will only face a one-year prison sentence for holding firearms. If one of them testify and the other does not, the one who testified will go free, and the other will receive a ten-year prison sentence, and vice-versa. If they both testify, they will both receive a three-year prison sentence. They have no communication with each other, making the situation complex for themselves. Putting them in a position where they must either trust their partner or save themselves.

The golden rule is to treat others the way we want to be treated. So if these prisoners follow the golden rule they will both choose to stay silent, hoping that is what the other will do. The point of the prisoners' dilemma is not to show us what our options are if we ever get arrested with a friend for robbing a bank, it's to show that if we have trust in each other we all get the best outcome. But the problem is that Tronte wouldn't believe that Torben will stay silent as well, so he decides to testify. He betrays a friend to save himself, because as humans we always look out for ourselves.

Most of the time we judge people because we fear they are judging us. We think they're going to testify against us so we do it as well. Instead of treating others the way we want to be treated we treat others the way we assume they will treat us.

Unfortunately, many of the problems we see in this world and in our personal lives are escalated through misunderstandings. Misunderstandings minimize the truth and lead to a more intense and unnecessary problem. We think a certain way due to the lack of trust. We don't act the way we want to; we act the way we feel we're supposed to in order to survive. No one wants to live in a world where they can't trust anyone. And I'm sure we all wish we lived in a world where the golden rule was really implemented.

It sounds so simple; treat others the way you want to be treated. Literally be the person you want others to be to you. Unlike Tronte and Torben, we're allowed to communicate with each other. We can show signs that we're not going to testify and that we're going to stay silent. It's like when they tell us that people become monsters when we treat them like monsters. The worry that someone is a threat leads us to feel insecure and make the wrong choices. That in turn pushes them to a position where they become a threat. I have been guilty of this many times. I would feel someone has something against me so I automatically have something against them. Sometimes our lack of trust can cause the very problem in the first place. A perfect example of this would be the misunderstanding between Mary Queen of Scots and Elizabeth II. Both put their countries into war due to lack of trust, when they had the capability to be allies all along.

I have had so many cases where my problems were created or escalated from misunderstandings. Who knows how different things would be if it wasn't for some of those misunderstandings. Something I realized though is that those misunderstandings that need to be cleared up will be, and those that don't teach us something else. My way of thinking and dealing with problems has put me in multiple issues of misconception. That is because people like to come to their own conclusions when they don't have all the facts. We're not always going to have the chance to explain ourselves because that's how life is. That's fine, because these are the moments we see who really knows how we are. When we think clearly and choose our actions logically, we then have the awareness that no matter how it's perceived we are in the right.

We all jump to conclusions, it's natural and common. But we should always give each other the right to explain, because too many problems occur from not knowing the whole story. Take the time to act, because so many times people around us could be our advantage but our uncertainty makes it the opposite.

If the arresting officer told Torben that Tronte testified against him even though he didn't, it would push Torben to testify as well. Again, unlike them, we have the opportunity to find out the truth from the source. Too many times we're ignorant. Maybe the conclusion we jump to could be correct, but wouldn't you rather figure it out for sure rather than make a decision based on something that could be wrong? We think it's not worth the trouble to get to the bottom of things. We don't want to put in that effort. Some people are worth the effort, and some problems are worth minimizing when we put in the time to fix it.

I hope I'm not losing you, and I hope you know that Tronte and Torben are representations of how we deal with each other in the real world. I know you like the names, they're cool, unique, and you don't hear them that often.

Most of the time the problem is created from the fear of an existing one, and if we all learn to let things unfold we'll see more solutions than misunderstandings.

So many things are blown out of proportion. Someone must have seen a nun looking out of a window enjoying the view, and they shat themselves thinking it's a ghost. They then go and make a movie about it and say it's based on a true story. I believe in ghosts and spirits; I'm not saying that they don't exist. What I'm saying is that Oren Peli might have just seen his curtains move from the air conditioning one night and got the idea to write about paranormal activity.

My point isn't to emphasize how disappointing the horror genre is when it comes to movies, this is to show you that most of the time problems are so minimal, and misconceptions make them seem huge.

One little piece of information can open the door to so many assumptions. I always wondered how I got into situations where things really got out of hand in terms of understanding what was really happening. As a person who thinks a lot, I like to believe that I have a strong mentality when it comes to perspectives. I also have an opinion of myself based on what I've experienced throughout my life and my way of thinking. I don't care about the opinions people have of me, and by people I mean those who don't exactly know me and would assume the type of person I am. I do believe that I live life right and that there have been multiple misconceptions towards me from other people. It's not a narcissistic way of thinking when you believe you're a good person who respects their decisions, because when you are you'll realize that most of the problems you face really are misconceptions. If you do your part right, then the problem is from the other person. But what makes this way of thinking not narcissistic is when we learn to keep it in our heart, rather than let it get to our heads. Believe it rather than think it. A belief is something you keep within and apply it to situations.

    Not everyone sees us the way we see ourselves. We cannot expect everyone to know how we think; what they see is what they get. We have all this knowledge about ourselves, and go crazy when people misjudge us because we are so certain that it's not true. There's a thin line between being in denial about our faults, and realizing that what we portray to other people just makes them see us a certain way. You can be the most generous person, but on one occasion someone you don't know very well saw you being selfish. Their perception of you will be that you're selfish. We have different groups of friends because different people trigger different parts of ourselves, but that doesn't mean that's all we are. It's just like the way of thinking; remember who you are so that's always the way you're going to act, when you do that you'll know that many of the problems you face will just be misunderstandings based on portrayal, eventually it will solidify and become natural. It's logical; no one can read our minds; they judge us from what we do. Do what you think is right even when there is no one around, ultimately we become that person.

    Working hard is important, but what matters even more is believing in yourself. Harry Potter said that in the context to motivate his friends when they were forming an army. I'm using it in the context where we should all trust that we are good people. We should disregard the idea that this world is not fair. Let us avoid the misconception the world taught us of being too cautious when it comes to trusting ourselves.

We should always remember everything to do with our own lives starts from inside us. Those of us who have been hurt by people were taught to remember that no one is worth you feeling pain, and we were comforted when those around us would tell us those who hurt us are not worth it themselves. Something I realized from my most recent betrayals is that it doesn't even matter who or what the person is. We shouldn't even spend a second trying to tell ourselves that they are bad people who don't deserve us. What we should remember is our value as a person, know who we are and what level we reached. No one is worth you doubting yourself.

We see bad things as bad experiences. Like what I mentioned a couple of chapters ago; just because things seem bad doesn't mean they *are* bad. We need to be reminded throughout our lives what we want, and who we want around us. Life always changes, it doesn't always turn out the way we think it will. We could sometimes think that people will be there forever and something would happen where they're no longer a part of our lives. When we realize that that's what life is about – having good and bad experiences to shape who we are – we accept these things a lot easier and avoid feeling the amount of pain we used to feel before, because now we see it for what it really is. Control isn't about telling yourself what should be done, it's showing yourself why it should be done.

The misconception that people have influence towards the way we feel is what invites all the negativity. We feel like they are giving us the license to be upset. So many times we've said "she made me angry" or "he made me do it", but it's like what they used to tell us when we were children; no one can make you do anything, we control our own choices. Real comfort and real happiness is when you're in control of the way you think and what you choose to act on, we should stop blaming people and start realizing that the amount of influence we have with ourselves is infinite.

It's easier to think this way when we're gentle. Being gentle is not weak, it is subtle strength. We really feel in control of ourselves when we're calm. Just because someone doesn't talk doesn't mean they have nothing to say. If you know what's inside of you and you learn to approach things with a gentle mind you'll see the mountain of solutions you'll come to, and even if these solutions take time at least you won't create any further problems. With all the good and bad experiences that we go through in life, being calm is always the best approach. Being calm slows down your body, and the more time we give ourselves to stay collected the better our approach will be.

I find that to be the trick when it comes to dealing with people and situations. When we work on ourselves and reach a point of comfort and state of calmness we're able to see that the negativity of others simply comes from that, it can be their negativity. By achieving a state of calm you are able to navigate the situation your way. We deal with things more logically and no longer have to worry about a certain insecurity: that we could be the problem. Insecurity leads to being defensive, and that escalates problems even further. By recognizing the problem exists outside of you and the people and/or situations, you are able to approach it with a clear state of mind and acceptance by assessing it logically and reasonably based on your core beliefs; your anchor. And if worst comes to worst and the fault is within you, at least we still responded in the best way possible. I see no disadvantages to being calm.

Don't misunderstand, I am not the calmest person in the world. Those who know me would tell you I can be hot headed sometimes. I recently came to this idea, and I want to make it clear that the idea isn't just being calm and approaching things calmly. You need to think about things from the start that lead you to being like that naturally. No one can just decide this is how they want to be and it sticks. This is why I emphasized the importance of realizing when it comes to your personality, we ourselves need to believe that we are capable of being calm. It needs to make sense. It's logical; when you think about yourself and what you've been through you see how you came a long way. You then identify your mistakes in the past and see how you want to move forward as a more composed person. We make our past mistakes a part of who we are going to evolve into and use them as strengths to improve the way we think.

People are unpredictable. We never know how or when those around us will change, because we don't exactly know what they go through. Something that we do know and stays constant throughout our lives is the knowledge we have of ourselves.

Many of us studied the persuasive triangle when we were in school. There are three techniques when it comes to persuasion; ethos (credibility and ethics), logos (logic and reason), and pathos (emotions and feelings). We've always viewed this as a technique to persuade other people, but the interesting thing is that the persuasive triangle fits perfectly when dealing with ourselves and our own problems.

We discussed logic and how it is the entire basis of the way we think. We don't want to live a life where we wire our brains based on something incorrect, it has to make sense for us to be assured we're on the right path. We all have a unique way of expressing our emotions. In many circumstances logic needs the assistance of emotion, as we live in an emotional world made up of human beings. Recognizing how we feel by correlating it with what we view to be the logical response strengthens our thinking in the current situation.

Ethics isn't about not doing anything wrong, it's about making choices. Own up to what you did and no one can use it against you. I would rather have the whole world know every single bad thing I've done and still make my own choices, rather than have someone use it against me and make my choices for me. The use of the persuasive triangle when it comes to our way of thinking enables us to take full control over our mind, allowing us to always make our own decisions.

The biggest misconception of life is looking for sources of happiness around us; trying to find things that make us feel better. The secret is that it's the complete opposite. When we find it in ourselves everything around us becomes something of our benefit. We think we have to convince ourselves of certain things to make us feel better, when all we have to do is look. No matter the circumstance, our control in the way we think is always constant. We always have the ability to set it to a standing where we know our worth and can differentiate right from wrong. If worst comes to worst and we see there are things that need work, at least now we know. Sometimes finding ourselves thinking about a worst comes to worst situation can be drastic and overwhelming, but when you enter each situation in the mental state of calm you know and can achieve, your worst comes to worst levels and you are able to make choices based on what is best for *you*.

When we reminisce about the past we sometimes see how much happier we were, and how comfortable life was. But that's a misperception. Just because we're at a harder level doesn't mean things are worse. It's perspective; learn to see the benefit, because even bad times pass by swiftly, or at least eventually. Would you rather live through it framing your life as scary, or exciting, or sometimes just plain stimulating? And when we do, we look back and can be thankful for where we've reached. There are moments I think back on and regret so deeply and I thank God that I've moved past them, and not only that but grown from them. This true understanding comes from the knowledge and capability of making the best out of every moment and letting go of regrets. This way of thinking only came recently when I applied the things you read before to my life. It works, if you don't think it does then great - but if you're still reading then I'm hoping you understand what I mean. Comfort doesn't require all the things we're led to believe that it does, all it needs is our brain and our way of thinking.

We know we're going to gain nothing by feeding into stress and negativity, except for stress and negativity. But with every situation we feel it's different and that this time we can't control it. It's always the shit, while our minds are always improving. So if you took care of it then, you can definitely take care of it now. We should have respect for our minds; not put it through tough situations and lose control. We owe it to ourselves to think of and consider every perspective.

Sometimes it could feel as though we are being selfish, or some might even call you selfish. It comes down to where your priorities in life lie. For example, people getting a divorce has a huge effect on a family. The amount of filters and perspectives affecting that choice can become insurmountable; Did they have children, do they share the same friend group, is one more loved than the other? Do they care what others think? Do they pretend to? The most common source of change is from relationships. I think. Don't quote me on this statistic. However, a shift in dynamic for any relationship is something that needs to be monitored while being adjusted, or else you find yourself in a situation that you don't feel safe and comfortable in.

Back to the example of divorce, from one perspective of a child. In my imagination it's something that is extremely difficult to go through to have your main role models in life split up. But if you realize that even though they're not together anymore doesn't mean they're gone, you see that things could in fact be better that way. You still have parental figures, they just don't happen to be together. As children we forget that our parents have their whole internal situations as well as their familial ones. With that you learn what kind of relationship you want to have in the future, choosing what kind of person you want to spend the rest of your life with. With it we also learn that things don't always work out the way they seem, but that doesn't mean it could be a benefit for the future.

One of the things we most misconceive in this world is the idea of normality. Most of the time we see things as normal because most people view it that way. Even when we don't believe it to be right, the fear of being ridiculed tempts us to conform. No one wants to be left out in the world, when really everyone is left out in some way. We all have our different ways of thinking, just because something is regarded as right by many doesn't mean that it's true.

Normal is Not Always Normal

In 1951 a psychologist named Solomon Asch conducted an experiment to investigate the extent to which social pressure from a majority group could affect a person to conform. Fifty male students from a College in the United States participated in a vision test. The experiment used a line judgment task, which is when the participants need to match one line with one from a group of three. Seven participants sit in the room, all but one of them are confederates. The one who believes this is an actual eye test is who they're conducting the experiment on. The subject is close to the end of the line, so by the time it becomes his turn he would have heard most of the group's answers. The associates had agreed in advance on what their responses would be when presented with the lines. Obviously, the real participant did not know this and was led to believe that all the others are participating as well. Each person in the room had to state one-by-one aloud which comparison line (A, B or C) was most like the target line. The answer was always obvious, but the people who answered before the subject all responded with the same wrong answer. Nearly forty percent of the time the subjects conformed with the wrong answers of those before them, and when debriefed they admit it was because of the fear of being ridiculed, and they knew the answer was wrong.

This is a well known experiment that conveys the effects of conformity we face in this world. You can argue that the subjects were just idiots for not being able to match a line. But we are guilty of conforming, because the idea of normal is so complex, we sometimes forget to live the way we want. The way we can ultimately choose to live.

What's interesting is that many ideas are considered normal because most people happen to think that way. It's not wrong to be different, we have seen many cases in this world where those who have the courage to own their differences have excelled in their lives. The point I am making is that sometimes we need to ask ourselves if something is right, rather than ask if something is considered normal. Because normal is not always right, it's just what is common.

People think that being open-minded is accepting everything; allowing that the things people choose to believe in is okay. People who talk against others' choices are labelled as closed-minded. The whole idea of open and closed minded makes us blind to what is really right and wrong. The example I am going to use is most definitely going to get a lot of controversy and some of you may get offended.

People can choose what they want to do in their own lives, they can do whatever the hell they want as long as they are not hurting other people. Many of you would agree with me but due to the sensitivity of this subject you'll find yourself reluctant to speak up. But this is in fact a problem we face in our world; we are born as either males or females, there is no other option. If your life led you to be sexually attracted to those who have the same gender as you, that's your choice. If you really believe that you were born into the wrong gender, and you feel you have no other choice but to do the surgery to change, don't advertise it. These decisions that people make should not be praised.

Our idea of modernity is not advanced, and the idea of open-minded is actually closed-minded. I don't know about you but I definitely don't want to live in a world where changing something natural is considered to be normal. There are people who face hardships that lead them to these choices, and most of these cases happen because of how the world normalizes this idea. We sometimes just think about wanting to be different and having the right to do anything that we fail to realize what kind of world we actually want to build. We can be so held up on something and not realize that it's not what we want. We should learn to emphasize the importance of being different and how to act upon it, rather than the desperation of it. Instead of just clinging to the idea that people have the freedom to do whatever they want, we should allow people freedom to live as they choose. Because ultimately, our minds are capable of incredible things. To be born into a world of magic through thought. It is the nature versus nurture debate: to be born something and become another. To be labeled as anything by another, unless it is for non-violent purposes, should simply be considered rude and unencouraged conversation. To have an identity, a complete identity, is a fallacy. As humans we are constantly changing, and on top of that we are living in a fast-changing environment. It's not waiting one week for the letter from a crush, it's back and forth conversations throughout the day. Immediate satisfaction guarantee. We are existing in a state of change so rapid it is affecting the way we progress as a society.

      Before, I didn't ask all of these questions. I didn't make assumptions. That wasn't right though. Life is a balance, and we are severely shifting it. How do you want to change? How do you want to evolve: with the world, or against it? Be cautious as to what we consider to be normal. At the end of the day, it comes down to work. Can we, in some primal biological state of mind, remember a time that we worked more for our lives than for our selves? Or vice versa? Nature versus nurture, mind and body. Why can't we realize it is nature and nurture, and mind and body. We are born from the unknown. We pass on, to the unknown. Why pit the very fabric of ourselves against each other? Why cause friction, why cause pain? Is it fear? Is it shame? Who brings the fear and calls it shame?

    Let's put these two together. Having others decide who you are and what you can be is their fault and their business. Having an identity and claiming it proudly for the world to see has power. Using that power for growth and knowledge and understanding can encourage a society where just because I was born a woman does not mean I have to live any roles assigned to women. Understanding and witnessing that there is a block in society with what I think can be demeaning, and unfair, and in today's world dangerous - depending on where you go. It comes down to allowing people to live as they want to live and not discriminate against who they are. I am definitely speaking from a position of privilege. I have the freedom (and time) to think this way. I have the audacity to claim how society should be shaped. Am I helping you? Right now, our lives are determined by privilege - in all its shapes and forms across all the cultures of the world. Being a male or female was the easiest and first way to tell us apart. And that's good for biological reasons, for nature. But not for nurture. Separating us and assigning us roles specific to gender is where it goes wrong. Right at the beginning. Allowing children to just be as they are, to grow into whoever they will be and remain respected in their societies is the only goal. Being respected, comfortable, and safe is our only goal. They can be who they want but they are still either male or female. Personal hobbies and interests can be diverse, but something as natural as gender should never be altered. Children already have a lot to consider when they grow up, gender should not be one of them.

    We've all heard the question "is the glass half empty or half full?". It's a common expression to indicate what a persons' view on the world is like. If they see the glass as half full they view things more optimistically, and if they see it as half empty then they're more on the pessimistic side. This is the general idea, when you're talking about a cup of water that symbolizes life over-all. I hope we all see the water as half full, if not I hope by the end of this book you will because life in general is absolutely amazing. However, sometimes we need to look at a glass of juice and see it as half empty. The point of the question itself is to demonstrate that situations are seen in different ways; we could see opportunity or trouble. There are things in life that when we want to see them as opportunities to benefit our world or if they may cause trouble, we can't just think of the glass of water. Not everything is divided into optimism and pessimism. We don't have to be pessimists to feel pessimistic towards something. It's actually the opposite; if we know what to view something as good or bad, aren't we reaching an optimistic goal? We all make up the atmosphere of the world. It's not being conservative or closed-minded when we disagree with something. The idea is that agreeing with everything is not always the right choice. Although individuals are free to do what they please, promoting it as something normal will just allow confused people to follow, because they believe that to be the norm. There are some juice flavors where we should see the glass as half empty rather than half full. Disagreeing does not make you closed-minded, going against norms that go against nature does not make you closed minded, we need to be smart and not just accept everything because we believe that is the solution to a happier world.

We shouldn't be clones in a world filled with possibilities. The meaning of difference is not acting out to emphasize to the world who we are, it's about realizing what's important in life so that we base our choices off of what we really want. What differentiates people from others is what they believe on the inside, not what we believe to be normal based on the information we gather around us. Take criminal law for example, as someone who has taken interest in the legal system I find it really ironic how the concept of criminal law is portrayed. The simplicity of it is to represent people in criminal cases and prove a persons' innocence. It's not a secret that in many cases in the world innocents are being sentenced to jail while some criminals run free, and this statistic is thoroughly fueled by privilege. The idea of winning and not caring whether or not your client is innocent really defeats the purpose of it all. Before you argue that the world is cruel, realize it is cruel because of those who conform to this stupidity. You don't have to be a lawyer to know what is right or wrong in this situation. Lawyers are those who have studied and excelled at studying right and wrong - arguably the most complicated way of thinking - and many of them find it normal to care more about winning rather than finding the truth. Their job is to find a truth that benefits their client, not society.

We see this shit all the time. The Central Park Five are five innocent men who were convicted of raping and murdering a woman in 1989. The events were portrayed in the series 'When They See Us'. Full disclosure, I never watched it, but I read up on the case. In this specific instance we see how easy it was for human beings to convict five young children, all below the age of seventeen, and send them to prison because of racism. Fact.

      I am an Arab who has travelled to many places, and spent many summers in camps abroad. I have experienced racism in its ugly forms and subtle ones, and I understand what it is like to feel discriminated against. I never let it get to me because we Arabs find it amusing when we're associated with such stupidity, which in a way is a form of privilege. I have been asked if I was holding a bomb more times than I can count, and I've also been called a terrorist. I know people who have been blacklisted from the United States because white college graduates claimed to be threatened by their existence, or falsely accused as a result of a joke. It became normal for people to feel cautious around Arabs due to the amount of "terrorist groups" that formed in the Middle East. I put "terrorist groups" in quotations because it is worth mentioning the definition of terrorism today has stemmed from decades of white supremacist ideals. The fact that the majority of these groups were originally formed by western nations to benefit from the destruction of Arab nations, how dumb do people have to be to associate an entire race with something like that. I'm not bringing this up for people around the world to feel sorry for those who face racism, I am bringing it up so that we can all realize that it's actually normal in this world to associate an entire community with stereotypes. President Donald Trump was a dumbass; does that mean all the American people are idiots? Black individuals are statistically more likely to be convicted of a minor crime than Whites are for a greater crime, is it because the Black community is inherently more violent? Or are we perpetuating a belief that has stemmed from oppressing communities in order for the majority to benefit? It is also worth noting that this happens *everywhere*. In every country there is a portion of the population that benefits from the legal, economic and social systems, and those that suffer from them.

The term racism and the idea of being racist makes us blinded to the most important fact on this Earth; we are all human beings who are capable of thinking logically, and with that logic we should realize that our world will be a lot better if we become better people. Also, we all die. It's that simple; if we all work together we all achieve what people believe to only be a fantasy; happiness. It's not just a fantasy, it's possible. It is achievable. I really don't understand why we invite these ideas that divide our world and create more problems. No wonder people want to go to fucking Mars. People literally want to go to another planet that has no life, and start a whole new world. That's where we are now. Horrendous.

Unfortunately, it's normal to accept the way things are. It's normal to not be different in certain situations because we have a human tendency to conform. Let's bring back the juice theory. I'm allergic to bananas, so for this case let's view it as banana juice. Disgusting. This is one of the things we should view as glass half empty, because it brings no opportunity to our world, it brings trouble. People discriminating based on skin color has been at an all time low for centuries. We no longer live in the times where we knew very little about human beings. We're not actually naive enough to genuinely believe that people with a specific skin color are less than others in society.

Have we not realized yet how ridiculous it is that people discriminate against others based on their skin color? Did you know that there are three times more white people who are charged with crimes than black people? It's not because white people are more violent, there just happens to be more people who are white in prison than those who are black. Why can't we understand that it's the person themselves that makes the choices, regardless of their skin color or nationality? When we disregard the idea of racism entirely we focus on the person themselves, and we should all work together to eliminate the idea of racial abuse in this world. Stereotyping is a cognitive representation of a social group to help simplify the social world. It was introduced to simplify our complex world because it disregarded the idea of holding space for each individual as themselves. What should be done is extremely simple: see everyone as a human being regardless of skin color, and gender as well. If we disregard gender roles, the psychological trauma that comes to individuals who don't view themselves as the gender roles they were born into would, theoretically, cease to exist. Humanity has come up with many ways to divide us and cause trouble. Racism is one of them, stemming from colonialism. Gender fluidity is an extremely human concept, however fitting it into society when it is different for each individual causes problems. There is a reason why those that are gender fluid are faced with hatred and skepticism: it's because we have always separated the man from the woman. Why should we believe we don't have the power to disregard these aspects of our world to build a better one?

People get demotivated to make significant changes in the world because they believe they shouldn't have to put in the effort for future generations. What we forget to realize is that our world is so much more connected than it ever was, and we have the ability to reverse the normality of discrimination and the views people have in a short period of time. The world works on the basis of how we think and what we do. It's logic; if we think good we do good, when we do good the world becomes good. Collectively, if we stopped procreating, we would eliminate the entire human race. Collective suicide. In my opinion, by not addressing these issues we reach the same end. Looking out for only ourselves or our in-group will lead to the collective suicide and desolation of the other.

I cannot emphasize this enough: We need to really think about what is normal and what is not normal. It's not normal to judge someone on color, say it out loud and you'll realize how absolutely absurd this idea is. It shouldn't even be an argument that there are Arabs who are not extremists or suicidal, it shouldn't be an argument when people say that not all black people are criminals and that they deserve justice. It should be a given. We need to naturally realize that we're all people no matter where we come from or how we look. For the world to naturally think this way, which is what we all claim we want to achieve, we should start with ourselves. Just like when dealing with our problems. Think about it this way; everything inside of us needs to work properly in order for us to function well. It's the same with the world; when we all do our part the world itself gets better. It's not that hard, and now that we are all connected more than we ever have been, we have the capacity to work together and see what we can deem as normal and abnormal. We have the capability of changing the way those in power have programmed us to think. We have access to change the status quo. Theoretically.

It's like when we think about governments and their policies. It's evident that in many constitutions some rules don't fit well with how our world is today. Just because someone wrote it down a long time ago doesn't mean it's right and should stay. The same is true with racism, just because someone deemed white people the superior race does not mean that man-made truth should be a part of our world. Things are normal when they are common, things are common when they are talked about. Each of us should see what we want to consider normal in this world, and I really believe that anything can be done in this world because it is filled with more good people than bad.

We should all learn to implement the three pillars of class to ourselves; love, morals, and discipline. By love I don't mean lust, but the unconditional love you feel towards your brother or sister. Have you ever loved someone so much that you'd do anything for them? Where being selfless was truly a selfish act and, even if it was a burden, it's worth it? *Love* yourself, and do what you can to make yourself happy. This normality of self-discrimination is what builds darkness inside our hearts. Love yourself, you'll forgive every mistake you make and learn to move on. I love myself more than you can imagine. I go out of my way to make myself happy. We're really good together, you should try it with yourself.

Morals are when you can differentiate between right and wrong. So far you've read two chapters of how I personally think of what is right and what is wrong. There is a lot of karma in this world, be good and you'll receive good. It really is that simple.

Lastly, *discipline*. The most important one; self control. When you're in control you choose what you can do. That's the first step when it comes to knowing what is good and bad. We need to normalize these things within ourselves so that we can portray it to the world in our everyday lives.

Another senseless trend in the world is how people portray their negative aspects as something to be proud of. I haven't had Instagram for months now, but the thing I remember is how much people promoted failure as something that is normal. People who label themselves negatively as though it's a sign of their own strength are just ugly people looking for an excuse to lean into their unpleasant nature. There is no benefit in putting yourself down. Yes, it makes people laugh - but there is a place for self-deprecating humor and self-deprecating coping mechanisms. When we were talking about misconceptions, I mentioned the importance of self-evaluation; building a path from within towards calmness. It needs to make sense. When we love ourselves we elevate ourselves. The best thing about checking yourself is that even if the worst comes to worst, and we see that we don't have the capability to think in a way that is beneficial to the self, at least we know that we have that problem. Like what every single teacher and adult used to tell us when we were younger; the first step to solving a problem is knowing it's there.

Let's make it normal to keep our mouth shut when it comes to sharing our troubles and problems, because we're only hurting ourselves. It's one of the three things I believe everyone should keep private, and these three things are; your income, your obstacles (problems), and your next move. There are things we do ourselves for ourselves. When we keep it inside and not feel the need to share then we know we really are comfortable with ourselves.

It's so sad how materialistic this world is. People focus so hard on how much money a person has rather than what they did to earn it. I am personally a lot more interested in the things people do rather than what they earn. I like to think of money as a tool, and we are each given a toolbox in this life. You can look at other people's toolboxes and compare it to yours, see what you don't have compared to what they have. You can do that, and people do. Whether you should is another question. A common phrase I like is 'comparison is the thief of joy'. And remember, we're talking about your perception of that person's toolbox - and also your perception of your own. Because of that I also like to think that our toolboxes are not all they seem to be: one day you may find you have a secret compartment, or that tool you have that seems to be of no use to you is the reason you never lose the entire box. Things people have, what they've earned, that's for them to enjoy after all of *their* hard work. Materialistic things are only to be used and cared for by the owner themselves. When you reach the point when you're not attracted to other people's toolboxes you'll know that you are comfortable and thankful with everything in your life. On top of that, the normality of obsessing over something as common as tools (money, goods, etc.) will seem ridiculous to you. Yes, money is a tool that can make your life easier, more comfortable, more luxurious - but it's how you use it that makes the difference. How many people have you met that think they are on top of the world because they have wealth? People who over promise and under deliver, because of the ease money gives them in life? You'll realize that the majority, if not all, of these people are the ones who have not done much to earn it. Those who work for it know that the importance lies in what you have done to earn it.

Never tell anyone your problems, half the people don't care and the other half are glad you have them. What's the point in sharing your problems anyway? There's a normality where people like to share and find it funny to promote failure, or that they feel it'll make them feel better. I was practically living with someone who had something to complain about every single day, and you really pity a person who can't see the best in things. You're hurting no one but yourself, and you'd rather deal with your problems alone without the need to share them. It's what you do in the dark that puts you in light. These are the moments of self reflection and self evaluation; overcome your problems by yourself because that way you gain the most out of it.

We all have our ambitions in this world and the means to excel in our lives. Note: excelling looks different for every life. It is not what you have done but how you have done it. There's no point in sharing what you do before you do it. I found that saying 'I did…' is a lot better than saying 'I'm going to do…'. Work in silence and let the success make the noise. No one needs to know what you're going to do unless they're a part of it. Sometimes we feel like we need to tell people our plans so that we motivate ourselves to do them, but that only makes us work with our tongues rather than ourselves. Besides the fact that we're just going to look like idiots if things don't work out – and there are times when things don't work out – we automatically forget the reason we do the things we do; it should be all for ourselves and not to impress other people. It's okay to think about how it will make you look to other people; these are from the insignificant things I mentioned earlier that should fuel your motivation rather than be the reason for them.

There's so much in this world that falls under confusion when we look at what is normal and what is not. In a connected world, we feel normality is the majority opinion. It's interesting to wonder if the majority of that majority only think that way because it's a majority. There is absolutely nothing wrong with being different. It's actually what highlights the uniqueness in our personalities. Our modern world allows us to see the way things work in the lives of people around us, and because we have too many experiences of too many people's lives it influences our own, and with that we no longer control the way we think. It's important to remember that just because we can share our opinions with people doesn't mean we should all have the same one. I would also like to remind you what I mentioned earlier about society: societies have always existed, thriving and falling in the cycle of life. Accepting what is normal based on what society says, and seeing that our "modern day society" has basically been plugged into an algorithm of how the world *should* be or *should* look - it all comes down to people in power wanting to simplify the greater population. So we become sheep. Be a sheep, but don't be their sheep. Don't be what a sheep *should* be, be how you choose to exist.

Social Media and Technology

Last September there was an army recruitment rally at Ahmednagar, and the registration began on the 9th of July. How am I aware of this? Globalization; the way the recent advancements of our world manages to connect all of us together in a variety of different ways. Disneyland opened the 'It's a Small World' ride in 1966, and if they thought the world was small then I wonder what they think of it right now. As a political science student, I have written more than twenty essays on globalization in the last three years. It's a dominating process of interaction in the political and economic world. What's interesting is that it has a greater effect on our social world.

In today's world, convenience is the leading factor. Technology has brought us all immediate satisfaction in ways past generations could not imagine. Science has progressed in such an unfathomable way and revolutionized tech to make our lives easier and more efficient. We no longer have to go down multiple stories using stairs, we can now use elevators. No one really leaves their house to pick up the newspaper anymore because you can read any article you want online. You don't have to go to the store to buy this book, you can just download it on Kindle. We communicate with our friends around the world with messaging or calls. These are from the most basic creations that have really changed our lives. We no longer have to carry signed pieces of paper from the bank, ApplePay exists.

Full disclosure: I love technology and I definitely love convenience. What I do not love is ignorance, and the following two chapters will discuss what ignorance is doing to our world and to the people in it.

There have been many cases where people complain about how our privacy is being breached, or that there are people listening to every conversation we have via microphone permissions we've given applications. We find ourselves freaking out when an advertisement comes up on our phone about something that was just discussed. We all allow our phones to enable microphone access; certain words that we say trigger the system and advertisements on the topic come up. If you're talking about wanting to get food from McDonald's, an ad for a Big Mac comes up. Yummy. Do we really think that with all these technological advancements, big corporations are not going to take advantage of things like this? The world is advancing, and so are these corporations. Actually, the world is advancing at the rate of these corporations. It is coming down to knowledge and influence, and who has it. We should be able to differentiate between what we need, what we want, and what these corporations are trying to convince us we need and want.

Something we should all know is that we're not all being overheard by some creep in the FBI. Honestly, if someone was listening in on my entire life – although they'll be entertained – then they really need to get a life. I believe that they can hear us if they want to and there may be certain words or phrases that alert them to listen in. If someone is repeatedly saying things that are linked to a current violent event happening in the world, then the authorities or whoever it is listening in might have access and find out who they are.

How many of you have read the terms and conditions of your mobile phone when you first activated it? In the terms and conditions of IOS 5, section four that is titled "Consent to Use of Data" explains how they have the right to have access to all of our information on our phones. The latest system software, IOS 12, has a similar section but worded a lot friendlier, and is more on the basis that they can if needed. What's interesting is that they have always told us that they have access to our devices. They don't care what we do on our phones, they're not that bored to go look and see what we do.

Since last year, when we open a website on our laptops or phones a pop-up comes out asking us to either accept cookies or cancel. They now ask us if we're okay with them having the ability to listen to what we say and keep track of what we search. That is because even though it has always been there in the terms and conditions people found it crazy that tech companies have the ability to hack our phones. These are the problems people focus on when it comes to technology. But the purpose of my book isn't to discuss information technology and the importance of cyber security, it's to emphasize the importance of self-comfort, and control the way external factors influence our way of thinking.

Social media platforms alone have an almost immediate influence on people's lives. We have welcomed all the advantages and conveniences they have given us and completely ignored the responsibilities and consequences that they bring.

Applications like Instagram, Facebook, or Snapchat are great ways for all of us to keep in touch. We share their experiences, we can talk to people who are in different parts of the world, and we can easily stay updated with our friends and family. Companies also take advantage of these platforms by either promoting their businesses or using it as a way to gather customer preference. It really has its conveniences.

There are two main issues when it comes to social media and technological interactions; how it affects our lives, and how easily it allows us to affect others.

Besides the fact that the addiction wastes an unbelievable amount of time, most of the time we're online simply to be online. Open your phone now and check your screen time. Look at how much time you spend on these applications alone. If it's not that much then good for you, but if it's more than a total of two hours a day then you know what I mean by waste of time.

Something I noticed when I deleted Instagram earlier this year is that everything I do and everything I see is a part of my life. I don't waste a minute looking at things that do not involve me. That is when I came up with the philosophy I mentioned in the second chapter. By the way, this phrase already existed before I thought of it, but I didn't know and came to it myself, making me co-creator; The desire to want positive experiences is itself a negative experience, and the acceptance of negative experiences is a positive experience.

I have seen people with my own eyes, and have also been guilty of it myself, that we look at what other people post and feel envious. We think to ourselves "why am I here doing this shit and they're there chilling". Before you come up with the argument that it's all fake and people pretend to be happy, it's not true. There can be some of those cases but that's so pathetic I'm not even going to discuss it further.

Those people we see actually are relaxing by a beach, or travelling to different places, while we are at our base doing work or attending school. Everyone in this world has their own life, their own timeline, their own extent of success and stress. We all do things when we're supposed to do them. The problem with social media is that there is too much knowledge of other people's lives, so we find it difficult to live ours because we feel like we are missing out.

In reality, we are not missing out on anything. Everyone has their own timeline, their own toolbox. Everyone does what they are supposed to be doing at that moment. While you are stressed to shit I'll probably be sitting on a beach watching the sunset. When I'm studying for an exam you're probably spending a holiday in God knows where. We all have our own lives, our own time, and we find it easy to compare our lives with others when they happen to be doing something we want to do.

The quote that *I* created and mentioned; The desire to want positive experiences is itself a negative experience, and the acceptance of negative experiences is a positive experience, perfectly describes how social media affects our lives. It's so easy to just open your phone and fantasize about other people's experiences, and doing that has us escaping our own. Imagine that. We have accepted living in a society where we actively seek out distractions and diversions of our own lives. I wrote an entire chapter about the importance of accepting our experiences, whether good or bad. Social media comes with conveniences but it comes with responsibilities to ourselves as well. We cannot forget the meaning of life; everything happens at its own time and we all live our own lives.

In the last six months I practically became a fish from the amount of time I spent in the sea, and could have made an entire album of sunset pictures from the amount that I watched. I'm not telling you this so you think "oh wow he's so cool he saw the sun set". I am, and I did many times, but that's not the point. The point is that I realized that living in the moment is a lot more enjoyable than constantly thinking about posting something for everyone to see. Don't misunderstand, I have nothing against posting. It's the reason people follow you, to see what you post and what you do. But as the world advances, so should we. When we see other people doing things while we are in times of stress, we need to learn to accept the timeline theory; there are over seven billion timelines on this Earth, and it keeps increasing everyday. Everyone has their own path, their own sense of time. Age is just a number and our experiences shape who we are. If we learn to focus on our own and not be influenced by others then we will appreciate both the good and the bad times of life.

    There's a reason there are more cases of people who find it difficult to enjoy their lives in this century compared to all the others that passed, and it continues to increase. I'm not telling you not to use social media or to delete these apps, all I'm trying to tell you is that we really let these things get to us even when we don't realize. It's a full-on platform that has the capability to affect the way we think. We always hear things about robots taking over the world. It's not because robots are smarter, we can fuck the shit out of them. It's because we have been easily manipulated with anything technological. As convenience is what we're after, we embrace all the good in these things but fail to see the disadvantages. Further still, we embrace the good they want us to see and very few seek out the good our technological advancements that are not advertised, that are more personal, and that can truly help propel us into a better state of existence.

Technology is already winning. The solution isn't to run away from it, it has already become a part of our world and has a lot of benefits. Let's go back to the fight or flight theory with the additional Omar area; there is a middle ground. We shouldn't get sucked into it and let it control our lives, and we shouldn't try to avoid it because it does come with advantages. I have not cut out technology and social media, I am not the kind of person that will give up my gym membership and PlayStation - but I learned what works for me and what doesn't. I have learned what truly adds value to the life I want to lead based on the love, morals and discipline I have for myself.

Social media is fun and can seem harmless at times, but the more time we spend on it the more influence it has on us. It's meant for entertainment, not to be a fixed part of our lifestyle. At the end of the day it's obviously your choice. However, the way I see it, is that it's a new concept, where all of us at this point of time are the first to actually live with all of it. We have no past examples the way we have them for other things, because it never existed back then. But I would rather take precautions than jump straight into it, especially when it clearly affects the way we think. Especially how it affects the way we look at ourselves, the number of people that have cosmetic plastic surgery done, the number of photos posted with a filter versus without a filter.

This brings us to the second way social media influences us, and it is the ability to become influential yourself.

Hiding behind a screen is so simple; you would say things to people you'd never dare to say to their face, it's a lot easier to swear at random people that you're gaming with than swear at someone you see in the store - to name a couple. It gave us a barrier and safety zone, but what we fail to realize is how much it destroys the barrier of others.

If you've ever played with me online, you'd know I wasn't exactly a saint. One of the things I noticed when you get into a heated conversation with someone you don't know online is that we would say anything to offend them. Most of the things we say we don't mean, some don't have meaning, and afterwards we think back and feel like shit for actually steeping that low. Arabs are called terrorists, black people are called the forbidden word, and the interesting thing is that most of the time it's not coming from a racist standpoint. It's simply to offend the other person as much as you can. This goes back to my point in the chapter on what is normal; because it has become a tool people use to their benefit. A tool that wasn't made by each individual toolbox holder, but a tool that was mass produced by racist people in power and distributed among the masses. For it to stop we need to work together to discontinue this tool.

Look what happened after Rashford, Sancho and Saka missed their penalty kick in the Euro Final. People took a racist approach. They were absolute idiots. Rashford's penalty was trash. Sancho was scared shitless, and I don't even know what Saka was doing there in the first place. They did not deserve all the racist remarks that the disgusting people on social media were dishing out. Yes, the three players who missed happened to be black, so fucking what? They did mess up, but *not because they're black.*

Karma is a very important thing in our world. When we do good we're rewarded, and everyone that has done something bad has been punished. What goes around comes around, and there are consequences to everything. Even when we see people bolting in life and they are shitty people, one-day karma is going to hit them hard. But who cares, focus on yourself and make sure your karma is nothing but good. If you do get bad karma accept it and own up to your mistakes. Social media makes it easy for karma to come around over and over again. I would even go further and say the modern day world we live in that is dominated by a western misogynistic approach of existing makes it easy for karma.

Social media has helped eliminate the idea of real karma and has made people experience extreme types of it. I am going to give an example, but I'm not going to use names. If God forbid someone from my family is ever involved in anything I wouldn't want their name revealed in someone's book.

In 2013 a sixteen-year-old boy was caught in a video bullying a group of younger kids. In the video he was seen pushing them around, calling them names, and tripping some of them to the floor. When that video was released people began to comment. Understandably, those commenting were sharing their disappointment and disgust at what they had watched. They were cursing at the bully for what he was doing, and showing their hatred towards him. People then began commenting disturbing messages; they started to propose that he kill himself, and that he doesn't deserve to live. Eventually, they found out what his social media account was, and many people began sending him messages of death threats or insults. Not long after the sixteen-year-old killed himself.

We have all done things that are as bad as bullying. We have all faced consequences for the things we've done. The reason I mention this story is to explain my next point; social media has destroyed the purpose of karma, and has made people think they have the authority to share their opinion no matter who they hurt. Like Batman, we can take it upon ourselves to be Judge, Jury and Executioner. Also like Batman, we don't have absolute power to be those three things. But people can give you that power.

It's so easy to troll. It's so easy to conform with a group of people against someone who did something we have all done at least once in our lives. Yes, what he did was bad, but he was going to get what was coming for him. Unfortunately, we passed judgement and forced a consequence that is a pretty high price to pay. And to think, I have been a bully at times - but because it was never captured on camera and broadcast to the world I was able to grow, learn, treat people better, apologize, and *live*. How lucky. Online users don't resist when it comes to taking a moral high ground and thrashing people they don't even know. We should learn to let nature take its course. Everyone gets what they deserve, we have no right interfering in the affairs of the people we don't know. Social media may allow us access to act as juror, but we have no authority being their judge or executioner.

The best thing about social media is that it assures us that there are more good people than bad. After the Euro Cup Final, everything on the news was about how unacceptable the racist comments are. Worldwide problems are displayed on social media in the form of seeking support from the public, and making everyone aware of the problems. Certain events around the world are brought to light for people to be given the opportunity to be a part of it. We see where many people stand, and we thank God that there is more compassion than hatred.

Something that really confuses me in this world is the moral compass people have on different types of issues: selective justice, selective alliance, performative alliance, etc. Social media is proof that the majority of people actually care. In the general sense, there are more 'good' people than 'bad' people. In 2016, Cincinnati Zoo and Botanical Garden in Ohio were infamous for the killing of one of their Gorilla's Harambe. A three-year-old boy climbed into the gorilla enclosure and was dragged by Harambe, one of the zoo workers shot and killed the gorilla. Social media platforms were filled with people talking against the zoo workers' actions and the killing, demanding justice for the gorilla. This indicated that they feel for animals and want to protect their rights. Others began to criticize the mother of the child, asking why the child was there in the first place - showing those who had concerns about child protection, and whether or not the boy had a responsible mother. Wow, people are so wonderful that they care for a single animal who was killed, and the protection of a young boy who was not looked after and was in a dangerous situation. I'm not being sarcastic. It's great we have people that are so considerate. In a world like this, we all need to be considerate. It also goes to show that generally when there is an issue, especially the most controversial, it comes down to who is being considerate of what. When Notre-Dame caught on fire thousands of people rallied to help and billions of dollars were funded to fix it. There's nothing wrong with that, I won't speak badly of a good deed. What I will speak badly about though, is ignorance. People. Are. Ignorant.

The Blind Spot

As I mentioned multiple times already, this world is literally our home and is made up of all of us. We're all human beings who have two goals; survive and be happy. Most of the time we're all misinformed. Whether that's because we're reading biased sources, or because the world is so ignorant of certain subjects that require our full attention - and that is because people are afraid to speak against things that are out of their comfort zone or scope of understanding.

On September 11th, 2001 New York City was hit with the most horrific event that has ever taken place in the United States of America. It was horrible. Thousands of people were killed, thousands of people were injured, and thousands lost friends and families. The loss and grief of the attack has been carried forward, even to this day. That was the first time the United States had seen the level of violence that takes place in Middle Eastern countries. On a scale regarding atrocities on US soil, it was awful. On a scale regarding atrocities committed by the US, it was normal. It's important to remember the level of seriousness does not differentiate based on where it happens. I am not trying to undermine the 9/11 attacks in any way, rather I am elevating the loss and grief that a great deal of countries have gone through to the same level - because for some reason we relate *most* as an international community when something is affecting one of the leading powers of the world. Americans claim there was a pre-9/11 and a post-9/11, and a great number of people agree from all over the world. But it wasn't just because we grieved with them; we feared what their grief would mean to the world as a whole.

People who are bullied constantly in school are just like countries that have faced violence for many years. Since they went through the extremes multiple times at an early age, and continued to go through them it is seen as normal for them to be hurt, or normal for them to be in conflict and war. Some countries are just always viewed as warzones, even as their societies are trying to pick up the pieces and start anew. Something to be made clear; no matter how much violence a country faces, it never becomes normal to them.

George Bush retaliated by sending armies to Iraq right after the September 11 attacks. American tanks were driving in the streets of Iraq and their military killed hundreds of thousands of Iraqi citizens. Imagine what would happen if Iraqi tanks were seen driving through the streets of New York, if the decisions in the past had gone in someone else's favor. The fact that war games are set anywhere but the US, that are made to show Middle Eastern countries as hostile and a prime place for conflict; people grow up believing that this is all normal. Some even believe they are wars they should fight in real life. Just under three thousand people were killed in the 9/11 attacks, and hundreds of thousands casualties died in Iraq. It is not a competition, and all grief is valid. But the magnitude of the grief must be proportional and those that have a hand in managing the grief end up resorting to revenge, greed, and control rather than active healing and collaboration.

Why?

Systematic racism and oppression. It always comes down to having a system that serves most and oppresses some. Always. We have seen it with the

BLM movement that exists because of white supremacist control and enslaving another race, the oppression of the indigenous people in Canada as their identities and culture were slowly being erased, the control of oil in Africa and the pollution that third world countries have to deal with because of first world luxuries and lifestyles, the oppression of the Palestinian people by the Israeli government. There are more. Much more. These are the ones that have come into my realm of existence and are the most important to me - I would like to disclose they are the most important because I have learned about them the most. But injustice anywhere is a threat to justice everywhere. And there is injustice *everywhere.*

    Social media has become an incredible asset. We are able to mobilize and educate each other, share resources and elevate oppressed voices - it's incredible. When George Floyd was killed it echoed atrocities that Black Americans have been facing since the dawn of mankind; white is better. When corpses of indigenous children were found in unidentified mass graves the ugliness of what Europeans had done in order to gain power and influence to create North America was gaining attention. The more and more we go back, we are faced with the truth: Those in power write history, and that history is taught. Those in power want to be the heroes of history, and so they become the heroes of our world. Those in power though, at the end of the day, were just people. But because an ideology was carried through generations and continuously enforced, we now have a population that follows those norms as absolute truths. And it is harming our world. Actually, it is harming our humanity. The world will be fine, it will adapt. Earth has existed far before we have and will exist far after we have perished. Did you know the statistic of how long humans have existed in comparison to the age of the world is something like, 0.00001%? And in that time we have managed to milk it, turn it sour, and feed the expiration dates to our children. It is shocking how blinded we are.

The atmosphere of this world isn't all bad. A lot of us have good hearts and a delightful approach to life. There is probably more light than there is dark in this world. However that light is being redirected to blind us instead of being distributed to enlighten all. Those who face violence and oppression are the ones living in bubbles of darkness that only we, from the outside, can pop. Just hating what is wrong is easy, anyone can do it. We always say that when given the chance we would do things differently, and yet even when people try we call them out for performative allyship, or not being politically correct, or canceling culture. We all live life with our own filter, and just because we don't see something the same way does not mean we are on opposite sides, especially when "sides" are also man-made. Why make this world a battlefield when it could be a playground? Why fight when we can negotiate and elevate our knowledge and understanding, Teach?

There is a surplus of "humanity has failed" posts and comments all over social media. Humanity has not failed. We're still far from failure. If we keep sitting around thinking that we failed, we're only going to get there faster. Before the political world comes the social one. Who makes up the politics of the world? Politicians. What are they? People. It's sad to see how people are so ignorant and cannot show their courage or strength when the time matters. I honestly have so much faith in humanity, because there is something about our biology that is truer than true: human beings have the capacity to love, to create, and we seek companionship and socialization. We're all good people who actually care about each other, but we have to remember it. We have to know what reality is, and know the real story.

I've been focusing on the broad theme but I would like to take this moment to shed light on a particular blindspot.

Something to remember: It is interesting that the darkest spots sometimes have the most artificial light shined on them, to show a different shade of truth.

Imagine someone breaking into your house, killing a member of your family and holding the others hostage. That someone puts you in a bathroom and tells you that you cannot leave, and that everything in the house is now theirs. Every few days they come into the bathroom and beat you and your family. One time the person comes in and shoots your father while you watch, and leaves him there for you to see. One day the person comes in and gives you some money. They tell you that they are buying your bedroom from you. What good is the money going to do when you're held in captivity? Clearly the person just wants to legitimize his filthy plans to take over your house. Your neighbors know what's happening, but do nothing. You can see the fear in your family's eyes. You have no idea what's coming next, who's next to die, or if you're going to live to see the coming year. The person changes the household name to theirs, and all your neighbors begin legitimizing it. The next 'negotiation' you have with the person is when they throw some more money onto you and tell you that your kitchen is now theirs. Eventually they're going to take over your whole house.

What a horrible story, right? So messed up on a level that it's not even good. It doesn't make any sense, and it makes you think how could this ever happen? Where could this happen? If you're an active ally of oppressed people around the world, a couple of places might come to mind. This script has more remakes and renditions than Romeo & Juliet.

It reminds me of the movie Saw. A slasher movie where a man dresses as a puppet named Jigsaw, traps a bunch of people in a confined area where they cannot escape, and brutally murders them while enjoying every minute of them being tortured. I believe that Saw creators James Wan and Leigh Whannel got the idea of such a psychopath from the notorious mass murderer and terrorist leader Benjamin Netanyahu. It all started from David Ben-Gurion when he founded the terrorist organization and occupied Palestine back in 1948.

Some history: The land of Palestine was where Muslims, Christians, and Jews lived side-by-side. In the beginning of the 1800s it was ruled by the Ottoman Empire. Theodor Herzl founded the idea of Zionism in 1897, and introduced the idea to turn Palestine into a Jewish state due to all the atrocities and racism Jewish people were facing across Europe. After the First World War when the Ottoman Empire was dissolved, the English wanted to claim Palestine. And, although colonized, Palestine remained Palestine. However, Former English Prime Minister Arthur Balfour wanted to kill the Rothschild ass so badly that he made a declaration in 1917 supporting the establishment of a Jewish Homeland in Palestine.

More and more Jews began to arrive in order to seek refuge from truly awful situations of racism, ridicule, and torment. The Palestinians were welcoming, the idea was that so long as their culture and their lives remained the same, where is the harm in opening your homes to people fleeing terror? Unfortunately, the terror piggybacked on to some Zionist ideologists and slowly but surely control and power was beginning to shift. In 1948 the terrorism in Zionism was exposed. They murdered their way into a state and named it Israel, and thousands of Palestinians fled in order to survive. I remember my grandmother telling me that they left their homes as though they were going out to the store, with no idea that they would never return again. My great aunt still has her key.

Does this sound familiar at all? Remember, the Holocaust was legal. People knew it was happening. Read that again: the Holocaust was legal.

Before the script of oppression for one people ended, the one for another people was underway. The aching wound that is the Palestinian identity and pursuit of freedom has been reopened and badly sutured so many times over the past 70 years, and we didn't have the most noble of surgeons. To this day, Palestinians who fled do not have a right to return, and the Palestinians that stayed but did not accept the Israeli government as their own are constantly terrorized in their homes, their schools, their place of worship, on the street, at checkpoints... They also have no right to fight back, and if they do are labeled terrorists themselves. Children of 12 have been murdered by IDF soldiers with the claim that they are part of terrorist groups and will lead the future of Hamas. What. The Fuck? And still, there are Palestinians who exist only to resist. The pigs in arms hold weapons their balls can barely handle, and they do not stand a chance against the Palestinian heart. The Palestinian spirit.

We romanticize the suffering of our people because we have reached a point of helplessness so profound it has passed down through generations. The collective grief that social media platforms ridicule and silence, that governments blatantly ignore, and that the UN barely signs a warning for is one that this generation is fighting to be resolved. May we finally reach the final stage of this grief, but it will only come with justice.

In their own land they suffer from oppression and are terrorized by the most inhumane apartheid system on Earth. It was not the first, but I very well hope it is the last. Too optimistic? Will we be able to catch these colonial regimes before they rip up the roots of a land to claim it as their own? Is there any place left to colonize, anyway? For most oppressed people there is no humanity, no respect for dignity, and people have the nerve to tiptoe around the situation instead of having an opinion. I picked this topic obviously for selfish reasons, I am Palestinian. But I'm sharing it in this way because I want us to look at something so controversial in the same way we have been managing our emotions with logic. Why is there such fear of proving a government wrong? Is it fair to fear what secures you? Is it logical? My goal by the end of this chapter is for you to see what is really happening if you haven't already. If this topic is just an eye-roller for you for whatever reason, I would ask you to keep reading. Amuse yourself. You've made it this far. Why follow the views of a state that preaches the protection of its people at the expense of another? Why is one human life valued more than another because of the choices their ancestors made regarding which religion suited them best? I read this thing once that said even the Muslims that Israel are currently oppressing were probably, almost definitely, once Jews. How can we enforce such violence on people? Where does it come from, this thrill of conquering and making something "mine", regardless of the consequences?

My first solution would be to de-coin the term anti-semitic. Even Islamophobia. Semites refer to both Arabs and Jews, we share a great deal of history and ancestry: using the term anti-semitic divides a people that are literally the same. Also, I firmly believe everybody loves Jews - except for the people who have been explicitly taught and brainwashed to hate Jews. The biggest issue however, with the term anti-semite, is it is immediately tied with Israel and international opinion of their government. Everyone loves the Jews; they gave us Seth Rogen, Adam Sandler, Mila Kunis, Google, stainless steel, etc. Anti-Semitism has nothing to do with it, and that word is so irritating to even say. Let's not feed into this idea of Jewish threat and their safety. No one is after the Jews, it's the Zionists who are the plague in this world. I really hope we all begin to see past the bullshit. And the bullshit here is everything they try to distract us with. Don't you see how ridiculous it is to even consider that Jews are threatened because people are speaking against Israeli crimes?

It's time for people to think simply and stop being brainwashed by political nonsense. Look how hard it is to get people to understand what is actually happening. I can write ten books on the terrorism that the Palestinians have been facing from those inhumane pigs, I can also go extremely political and add specific facts and cases. I mentioned many times how we all make up the world's atmosphere, and the fact that something like this is happening and we all seem to be able to go on for years and years not doing enough is disappointing, and frankly extremely terrifying.

Thankfully, our world has more good than bad. That is shown during Palestine's darkest times. Instagram, Twitter, Facebook; all of these platforms are flooded with people sharing what is happening and speaking against those acts. Of course we find people supporting the Israeli terrorist group, and these people are either ignorant and brainwashed or they're just as much pigs as the rest of them.

That was the reason I mentioned globalization in the previous chapter, and why I went on to explain the importance of knowing the consequences of social media and how we should learn to control it. We have ways to communicate with each other and help the world see what is really happening. News on fucking Instagram is more reliable than news agencies most of the time. There is a correlation between political globalization and social globalization. Social globalization could be the best thing for this world, but unfortunately, because we all love to bring culture into everything, we seem to be getting nowhere. This is not a cultural thing. I am not telling you this because I myself am Palestinian. I am telling you this because it's shocking to see that a world with people who are capable of thinking logically has a terrorist group occupying a country, and have managed to legitimize themselves by making us all ignorant of Palestinian truths. Facts and truth swept under the rug to make way for a convincing narrative. And it is convincing. Jewish people have every right to be protected, but what kind of protection comes at the cost of a culture and population? A world of colonizers does not aid our humanity. That is the clearest message I have seen during the pandemic.

I want to make that clear, this is not just my opinion; these are facts. It's not something to be argued about. Besides the fact that I don't know you, I would never enter an argument when I'm not going to change my mind. I am a very reasonable person who has a very open-mind, and I hope you do too. Because with that open-mind you'll see that this is not a joke, and it shouldn't be a trend where people talk about it for a couple of months then forget. We need to stop recognizing them as a state, people need to wake the fuck up. If I was Reuvin Rivlin or Isaac Herzog, and I see how the world around me is turning a blind eye to all the violence my terrorist group is committing, then I'm only going to feel more powerful and more dangerous.

I honestly have no idea what the leaders of Arab nations are doing about this matter. I would love to get in a room with them and have a discussion on this, and I hope one day I reach that goal. I would rather live in a world of peace, even if it requires some war to get there, rather than live in a world of ignorance.

Many argue about how Palestinians have formed Hamas and that has brought more violence. Their country is being overrun, their families are being killed, you're wondering why or how a group has been formed to fight back? It is what it is and there is nothing wrong with it; Palestinians are fighting back, and they are using violence because that is what Zionists use on them. No one is helping them, you expect them to just sit and take it? It's so frustrating when people use Hamas as an argument to defend the Israeli terrorist group, and say that they are bringing violence. You can't just slaughter millions of people and feel threatened when they form a group against you.

Do you know what it's like to be a Palestinian not living in Palestine? You can't be bothered the way you should be, because every time you do, you realize how you live a peaceful life while millions are seconds away from death at the hands of terrorists everyday. There are Palestinians facing hardships and have been facing them for over seventy years, and there are Palestinians who see what is happening and wonder why no one is doing anything. My goal isn't to convince you to jump to team Palestine. So far everything I told you is the basics of the issue, and it should be more than enough for you to realize we are living in a world where we have allowed the largest and most powerful terrorist organization in the world to live among us.

We even turn a blind eye when one of them makes their way to our television. Imagine seeing Osama Bin Laden or Abu Bakr Al Baghdadi driving cars with Vin Diesel in the Fast and Furious movies. It's not about culture, it's about who the people are.

Omar ibn AlKhattab entered Jerusalem as a conqueror, he gave all non-Muslim citizens the freedom of religion and treated them well. Jerusalem has been captured and recaptured at least twenty different times, and has been claimed by empires and armies. There is so much controversy about who originally has claim to the land of Palestine, and the truth is that Palestinians do. Palestinians are made up of Muslims, Christians and Jews. Zionists are just inhumane terrorists who kill for their own amusement. Have you seen any of the videos of how Palestinians are treated? It boils my blood to see, not because it's horrific or traumatizing, but because it's actually happening and has been happening for decades. Palestine is Palestine. Zionism is terrorism.

A long time ago hundreds of people could be butchered and barely anyone would know about it. Today, one man could be killed and the whole world would not stop talking about it. That's great, it really is. It's a good thing that we are all a part of things that happen around the world. What sucks is that we seem to put in more effort when a church in France catches on fire than situations like this.

Remember how if we don't like something we should change it, and if we can't change it then we change the way we think about it? A country filled with innocent people is being occupied by a terrorist group, and the reason they are in power is because the world allowed them to be. It's not a stretch, it's not me living in a fantasy hoping that everyone gets on board. It's a goal, and it can be reached if people have the courage to make a change when something is not right. Most of the time, the reason we see things as unrealistic is because we're too scared to do something, and this is one of those times.

Daesh is a terrorist group that attacked multiple cities in Europe. Apparently they like to go by the name ISIS – Islamic State in Iraq and Syria. They don't represent Islam; the same way Zionists don't represent Judaism. The Israeli brainwash is the exact same as the Daesh one, the only difference is the world did not legitimize Daesh, and thank God for that. Because those people are just as sickening. Terrorism is not only linked to one religion, let's stop with that stupid fallacy. Besides the fact that the United States government formed most of the terrorist groups in the Middle East, the violence these groups bring were fueled by oppression. I am in no way defending them, but it's sad to see how terrorism is immediately linked to Islam while those who commit acts of terrorism in the west are branded as clinically insane.

The fact that millions of people have to post on their social media accounts just for people to understand that everything that was fed to them is bullshit, and that I felt the need to add this chapter to a book about living comfortably shows that this world is ignorant and does not realize that with ignorance comes consequences. We may feel like there's nothing we can do now, but there is. And with time it keeps getting harder and harder, but never impossible.

Speaking of the United States, I love the country itself. New York? Wow. What a city. It literally has everything, even a sour patch store. Hollywood has brought us the best entertainment, and also triggered Bollywood which is pure comedy no matter what genre they try to convince us it is. There are so many things in that country that benefit us. But the one thing that everyone can agree is negatively influencing our world is the government. The United States was established in 1776. Before that it was just Europeans who migrated to North America to either escape their crimes or start a new world. Either way, the United States doesn't have an actual history. They have no cultural identity as they were formed by Europeans who took over the land from the Natives.

Did you know that Christopher Columbus thought he had landed in what we call Indonesia today? Back then it was called the Indies, which is where the term Native Indians came from.

No historical cultural identity, and that's fine because they managed to build their own culture over the years. But that is why they are always acting like Judge and Jury when it comes to the problems of this world. The United States government tries so hard to make their mark on the world by constantly getting into the business of other countries, and I hope a lot of people see through it as well. What's sad is that many countries have been destroyed in the short-term to benefit the United States. The Taliban was actually created by them, and after all those years of fucking up Afghanistan because they were 'trying to help destroy Taliban', the Taliban has resurfaced and continue to terrorize Afghanistan today.

It's no secret the media is not exactly free with their speech. It's not the complex way we think it is; that the media is secretly controlled by the government. It's right there in front of us, of course it is. But something I found interesting is that when you know enough about a situation, even the most biased article can be seen through. There is information that they give us, and there are facts that are in front of us. It's really not that hard to tell the difference.

"Palestine will be free". We've seen this everywhere, and it is true. One day they will be free. It's a bit annoying that I am excited to see the day when everyone wakes up and humanity kicks in. Mordechai Vanunu, the nuclear technician for the Israeli terrorist group realized who he was working for and went against them. Let's wake up before it's too late.

Do you ever get these moments when you remember something from when you were a child, and remembering it with your way of thinking now you pick up on things you didn't pick up on before? When I was nine-years-old, I went to summer camp in Switzerland. I remember I met a lot of people who were from Israel. I was nine, so the whole issue on Israeli terrorism wasn't exactly clear to me. But there's something I remember and I will never forget; once we were lining up for one of the activities, and there was a boy named Zack. Zack lived in Palestine, and obviously since misguided by his parents, he called it Israel. One of the counselors obviously knew I was Arab from my name, and I remember so well that she asked him where he lived. When he told her, she looked right into my eyes and asked him to say it again. I had no idea what was happening, I didn't think anything of it. But I remember her saying "he lived in Israel" more than four times while staring right at me. When I was gathering the ideas of this book I remembered it, and it made me realize how disgusting people could be. Someone tried to make a nine-year-old feel like shit. That idiot didn't realize I was only nine, and didn't understand what she was talking about. But still, that is when I realized how absolutely fucked up people can be. And I would rather go out of my comfort zone to try and do something about it than live ignorantly.

    People post, people write articles, take part in debates, and even hold space via support groups. Although smaller communities have been making some headway, globally the shift is taking longer than it should. We see the atrocities happening around the world and our response is severely lacking. I have seen people shed light and want to do better, but I have also seen people shed light and move on. I have seen people sweep the information under the rug and move on, and also know of some who sweep under the rug but do better. Based on how we view the situation and how afraid we are of the consequences, it is near impossible to have a united response. The media has been weaponized to divide like-minded human beings across all cultures about issues based on labels and societal norms that are man-made and therefore imperfect. Social media has made it easy to engage authentically with others around the world to establish proper dialogue and discourse, but it has also opened the gateway to trolling and online bullying. We are complex individuals who make decisions every day, but are we being held accountable for them? We are being told how to think, what to think, and why to think it. The aim of this book is to break down these structural oppressive norms so we can all begin the journey of true existence: in harmony with each other and the world we call home.

We can think back to the persuasive triangle. Logos are used when explaining exactly what is happening and that something is not reasonable. It's logical to know that the Israeli government are in fact terrorists who have been terrorizing the people of Palestine. With ethos we see that this is morally incorrect: the slaughter of innocents and driving families away from their homes is definitely unethical. We see many photos and videos of what the people there are going through at the hands of these terrorists. With pathos, we feel like shit when we see these things because it's hard to see the way people are being treated in their own homes, and in front of their own families. It's hard to think this could have easily been my family if my great grandfather decided to walk west instead of southeast.

All three parts of the fucking persuasive triangle explain how everything these terrorists are doing is wrong, and I know for a fact that their time will come when they face their consequences. I hope we're all on the right side of history when that happens, I hope we all prefer to go out of our comfort zone so that when we achieve what we want to achieve we're in a better place than we were before. I spoke a lot about our personal problems, and I mentioned how the world has its own, and this is the biggest one it has. Let's stop being ignorant and learn to see that. By highlighting the impact of colonialism and domination, by encouraging people to live harmoniously instead of selfishly,

I find it ridiculous how the topic of Hitler is considered taboo and rude conversation when the Israeli terrorist group is literally mentioned everywhere as a civilized and legitimate state. Hitler burned around six million Jews amongst other crimes, I am in no way trying to undermine that. But the extent of the sensitivity around that topic compared to what Palestinians are suffering in the hands of terrorists is extremely ridiculous. Things are improving. The world is beginning to understand. It's going to take time, that's the consequence of years and years of ignorance. But it will happen. For those of you with a functioning head, don't argue with people who try to defend the terrorists. Don't waste your time. Don't enter the argument if you're not willing to change your mind, and do not feed into their bullshit. Because they either know they're wrong and are trying to bother us, or they are completely deluded. Either way, let's focus on the main issue rather than what these animals try to justify.

I realize the book took a bit of a dark turn. This is our world and a part of it is getting slaughtered by a group of terrorists that have managed to display themselves as an actual country. It's really important to always remember where you came from. No matter where you go you need to remember your base. In situations like this it's important to remember that we all share a similar base; the world. Even though I do not see in front of me what is happening, I know. And you all know too. Let's not be ignorant.

The anchor and compass you see on the cover of this book is a representation of remembering where you come from no matter where you go. But I found another meaning to it which is actually the basis of my entire book; wherever situations take us we should always remember that base of thinking we developed in order to overcome our situations. It's literally a compass, not a moral compass, but a logical one. Wherever the environment takes our mind, let's remember to look at that compass and bring ourselves back to the position where we make our best decisions, and anchor ourselves there when dealing with the problem. Trust me, life is a lot more enjoyable when you make the best out of everything, obviously.

It's More Fun to Be Happy

It's all about perspective. There is so much more good than bad in this world, we just forget to see it sometimes. Some of us even choose not to see it, whether because we want to fix the bad or because we have been traumatized into believing we cannot be happy if the world is bleeding is up for debate. We live on an amazing planet, with amazing people who make everything enjoyable. I mean, Italy alone is heaven. From everything that we have been through we get to choose if we want our general sense to be a positive or negative one, and like I mentioned throughout this book it's all about how you think of it. The thing that triggers all of these shitty emotions is stress. We all feel it. Some of us deal with it better than others, but we're all capable of controlling it or eliminating it as a whole.

Imagine a cup of water that is nearly filled to the top. If you pick that glass up for three seconds, does it feel heavy? Obviously not. If you pick it up and hold it for five minutes, is it starting to feel heavy? Maybe a little. But if you hold it for an hour, your hand will start to cramp. If you hold it all day long your arm is going to feel paralyzed. The weight of the glass doesn't change, but the longer you hold it the heavier it feels. Stress is just like that glass of water. If you think about it for a few minutes it doesn't bother you. If you think about it for a while it begins to hurt. And if it's all you think about you'll feel mentally paralyzed unable to do anything, haunted.

We should always remember to put the glass down, and we always can because stress comes from within. If there's something we learned from this book is that we can always control what comes from within. Sometimes stress can be a little too much though.

Some people get diarrhea from the amount of stress they're feeling. Stress can manifest itself physically, but instead of seeing that as a hindrance we should use it as a clue. Our bodies are the maps of our lives, and by finding out where we hold tension in our day to day lives we can work against it - stretching, yoga, breathing. That is the way to put down your metaphorical glass of stress.

Time passes. Yesterday went by, and we're here now. Happiness isn't about not having problems, it's about learning how to control them and knowing our priorities. I found that the way to truly be happy is when the good things in our lives make the bad things seem pointless. We all have problems and we'll always have them; it's all about perspective. Just because things are the way they seem to be doesn't mean it's the way they should be. I don't just mean that when it comes to misunderstanding a person or situation, it's when we misunderstand the idea of being happy. There's nothing wrong with having a positive view of yourself, it's the best thing we can do for our mentality. When we reach that level of comfort, our problems will still be there but we learn to put the glass down immediately, or even chug that shit. That's when we realize nothing is worth the worry. Love your brain to the point where you won't allow anything to bother it. It already has its obstacles in the things we face so tell stress to fuck off because it's the last thing we need.

The first to apologize is the bravest, the first to forgive is the strongest, and the first to forget is the happiest. Knowing we're wrong just means that we have the ability to understand our strengths and accept that we make mistakes. We're secure enough with ourselves to take the hit. That's why it's bravery, because we built the strength inside of us that no external factor can affect. When we forgive we realize it's the other person's issue. We're logical enough to know that we stand by our actions and that sometimes people make mistakes. Forgiveness isn't a chore, it's a gift. Don't misunderstand though, it's not a gift to the other person but a gift to yourself. When we forgive we subconsciously accept that people have faults and that we understand where it's coming from. Forgiveness is by far the most rewarding thing you can do. I would change the word forget to 'move on'. When we've been wronged and find the strength to forgive, we should never forget, because we should always remember that betrayal exists. We move on because it's heavy to hold a grudge, especially for someone who we can choose to no longer affect our lives. When someone wrongs you, you should respect yourself enough to realize they're not worth you feeling a second of pain. We can forgive, but we must always remember. I forgive you, I won't forget, but I forgive you, because you're not worth hating.

    We're always around people. Especially now that we've come out of a year of isolation, we're seeing as many people as we can. Thankfully, most of us have been getting vaccinated for the last few months so it's making it possible to see each other safely. I had a turning point in my life and it took an entire year to get there. In that year I have gone through so many different stages. With all of them I recognized that things really go on better when you accept each situation and are comfortable with your choices. You really understand what it means to be happy. I should have made this clear from the start, but when I say happy I don't mean smiles, sunshine and rainbows. What I mean is personal comfort and personal satisfaction that whatever happens you are strong enough to not let anything affect you. Not only is your mood better but the situations you face are a lot simpler and clearer. We learn to see the best in people, and when we do that we benefit from everyone we meet. I would even argue to say true happiness is private - it's just for you.

I have met a lot of shitty people. I was always told when I was younger whenever I got into a problem with someone that I would meet people a lot worse in my life. I continued to meet shitty people, but those I came across when I was younger were just as bad; Emma Dhesi, Abe Lahmidi, Amy Kimball, Marilyn Malofy, the list goes on, trust me. But that list stopped when I realized that not everyone has to be your best friend. There is always at least one good thing about someone. It's a lot easier to see the best in people when you're not thinking too much about it. Like I've been telling you all along, there are so many things we can't change so we should choose to appreciate what we can. It's a lot better that way.

We were always told that if we fall we get back up. Sometimes when we fall, like literally fall, we get up and feel a bit dizzy. It's the same with problems, when we fall, we get up and our mind is all over the place. There's nothing wrong with staying down an extra minute. Reorganize our minds to the structure we want it to be in order to think logically. Everything is so much better when we control the way we think. It's worth that minute staying down for us to stand up stronger when we do get up. When we take a hit we're hurting, and it's very important to never make life changing decisions when we're hurting.

I swear life is so chill when you accept that things just happen. But you don't stop there, you accept and think about it in a way to achieve something. It's literally a win-win situation with yourself. We literally have the choice to smile afterwards or find ourselves more problems.

Because of how overwhelming problems can be, we sometimes think that there's no way out. Some of you may think everything in this book is bullshit, and that you cannot control the way you think in some situations. I don't care about how people can view this negatively, because happiness is real and it's here for us to have. Unfortunately, we were always taught that it's a reach and it's unrealistic to achieve overall happiness. We need to understand happiness isn't perfection; it's the power one has over themselves to make the decisions that fit best.

I am done letting the feeling of stress and the stages that lead to depression be the dominating factor in this world. Because of how many times we heard that the world is cruel and dark, we began to believe it. If everyone, or at least most people in this world aspire to find happiness and comfort, doesn't that just show that it's something that can be achieved? It all starts from each of us, from me, from you, the way we think, the things we choose to feel, and how we decide to act. If fucking Middle Earth achieved peace why can't we? Look at the US: systematic racism, ridiculous abortion laws, corruption, greed - and yet it is home to some of the happiest people, some of the most successful people: they have sold the idea of the American Dream. Sure it's not the most realistic dream, there are problems ingrained in it's very foundation - but success is achieved by seeking this dream, seeking this happiness, and wanting it for the world is, in my opinion, how we can reach global happiness.

Johnny Depp played excellent roles over the years. Easily one of the greatest actors of all time, up there with Leonardo DiCaprio and the entire cast of

The Inbetweeners. He was a great Gellert Grindelwald, but unfortunately his time was cut short due to accusations against him. Before all that madness, when he performed excellently in the second film, he said "the disapproval of cowards is a praise to the brave". In the movie he meant it in the context to convince someone to do something that people were against. But in the context of this book it fits well when it comes to the meaning of self-comfort. When we reach a certain level of being proud of our thinking any form of disapproval will clearly show where it is actually coming from, whether it is a misconception or someone with a problem, and we begin to see the bigger picture.

Something that is important to remember is to separate arrogance from confidence. I found that very difficult sometimes, and many would agree. Our sins are more dangerous than our enemies. That is the point of bravery when it comes to apologizing. We're all going to make mistakes, and when we see our own mistakes as our biggest problems rather than other people, we learn to accept our consequences and identify when we actually made a mistake. Pride is not about being in denial of your wrongdoings, it's about owning up to them and using them as a tool for improvement. Only then will our weaknesses become strengths. We own what we do because it's not about never doing anything wrong, it's about making choices. Happiness is when we make our own and comfort is when it becomes a natural way of life.

Like I told you at the very beginning of this book; I don't think of myself as the savior to the world. I have no doubts that people have better ways of thinking than me. But I realized how the shadow of the norm is casted on our happiness. Because of all the years that came before us things seem as though they're set in stone. Just because something hasn't happened before, or that we are used to seeing the way things are doesn't mean a new way cannot be created. Forget about what people say is 'unrealistic' or 'impractical'. I think the most important thing in this world is for us to be comfortable. Because when we're all comfortable everything else falls into place. I'm really not the type to sit and promote peace and want everyone to start holding hands down the street, but I am here discussing all of this with you because I feel the world is a lot darker than it should be. We spend too much time worrying when all we have to do is take a step back and see the logic in everything. Too many pleasures go by because we think worrying requires our attention, when in truth it's just wasting it.

Problems after problems, more and more stress, it's all never ending. We should learn to accept it, and accept that it doesn't mean we have to feel bad just because things are bad. The bad things in this world happen to help us appreciate the good. Not everything can be perfect all the time. First of all, life will get extremely boring and second, the point of all these things is to test us and increase our strength when it comes to the way we think. Think about all the problems you faced. Remember that dumbass before the problems happened. We have all come a long way. We get smarter and smarter with more trials. So let's use that smartness.

We spoke about misunderstandings. Have you ever been in a situation where it was a close call and if a misunderstanding had ended up happening you would have been fucked? Same. These close calls remind us of the fragility of understanding. When we see how things could have gone a lot worse then they did we open our eyes to how important communication actually is. Most of these near misses happen because we don't take full advantage of what we have in front of us. We waste our ability to think logically and spiral situations out of control. It's a shame if we continue to live life in a dark sense when there's so much light to enjoy. It's no secret that when we want something we fail to see what we have. Let's remember to look, because so many times forgetting to do that can really escalate something out of nothing.

My mother started saying a phrase to me recently, I have no idea where she got it but I loved it; waste not, want not. The first time she said it to me was when I left a half-full bottle of water on the table when I was about to leave the house. The idea of wasting water is extremely sinful to her, as it should be to all of us. But I started to realize that it applies to literally everything. It's like that quote I probably mentioned five times already; The desire to want positive experiences is itself a negative experience, and the acceptance of negative experiences is a positive experience. When we waste our time thinking about how we came to a certain point we get a desperate want for things to be better. When we waste our experience and fail to make the most of it we'll find ourselves steeping lower and lower.

Accept the things you cannot change, have the courage to change the things you can, and have the logic to know the difference.

If we waste situations we see that it leaves us wanting something to satisfy the pain. Grabbing it by the balls allows us to flourish in these situations.

Make the best of everything and you'll see how fun life could be. It's like when we wake up from a nightmare. I honestly love nightmares. So much fun. You're literally experiencing something horrible, facing a fear that scares the shit out of you. What's great is that you do all that and you don't have to face any permanent consequences, because none of it was real. We wake up and we're back to our regular lives. That big ass goblin that was chasing us doesn't exist, those half-men half-fish things on horses aren't trying to kill you - it's great.

It's not just about knowing, it's about realizing. A simple example would be getting over an ex. We tell ourselves we're better off and that it's their loss. But when we actually think about us and our mentality in the long-term, we really see that not everything works out. We see that although it sucks that it's over, it wasn't for us. We enjoyed every moment, learned from the things that hurt us, and now we can move on emotionally and mentally - hopefully stronger. You know when they say don't be sad it's over, be happy that it happened? Don't be happy, be grateful. Not everything is something to be happy about, but everything has a benefit, so we should consider ourselves lucky that we got to experience something. In the context of an ex we should definitely be grateful it happened; have you seen The 40-Year-Old Virgin with Steve Carell? Fuck that. Make every bad experience a good one. We all have the ability to do it, so why not?

We are indirectly taught to live the same routine and think a certain way. The idea of right and wrong became so complicated that we are blind to the fact that it's extremely simple. Mental health is not supposed to be a challenge. Life is already difficult. There are too many situations that we have no say in. So control the way you think. It's your mind, and it's you who will benefit from having a clear one, as well as the people around you. There is no reason to not be happy. We think reality is stopping us when it's really the bullshit that is. I know I repeat the same point a few times, all I'm trying to do is drill it into your mind. It shocks me that the solution is that simple, and it's disappointing that we were always led to believe that the world is a shitty place.

I'm going to say this again; if we want to build a better society in our world, we need to fix ourselves first. I used to think Gandhi said this, I tried searching it up but didn't find it online, so who knows who said it: "how do you expect to find peace in the world if you can't find peace in your heart". This quote supports one of the major points of the book. To build a better world – a world that is made up of all of us – we need to start by building a better inner self. That is the only way we can have any form of hope in a greater world. The first step in doing this is learning to overcome our own problems, we literally just have to do our own part. I really want to live in a world where everyone has a sense of comfort, let's work towards it. Let's realize that there's no way to help others or the society around us if we still haven't helped ourselves.

Life is black and white, and we're all grey. That ratchet movie told us that there are fifty different shades of grey, there are actually many more but who cares. The point is people face different forms of black and white, sometimes we experience the same black and white, but we approach it differently. It's the same when it comes to emotion; we feel the same types but approach it in different ways. And that's dependent on our past experiences.

At the same time many of us face the same problems but are affected by them differently. It only makes sense. If we watch a movie together, the same movie, and that movie highlights a certain theme that means more to you than me, you're more affected by it. It's the same in life, some of us are more sensitive to things than others. There's nothing wrong with that.

We all have our soft spots; we all have our weaknesses, and with that come our strengths. The point is to understand them because that is when we turn those weaknesses into strengths.

At the end of the day everyone in this world wants the same thing; comfort. It's evident that life is a lot simpler and happier that way. Don't be blinded by the negativity that has expanded in this world, because it's an illusion that casts a shadow over a beautiful world. Watch an episode of Tom and Jerry, eat a cheeseburger, do anything. The little things are what remind us that everything is not as bad as it seems.

We call these things 'distractions', but they're actually part of our lives to keep us moving forward comfortably. Boredom indicates the lack of use of inner resources; you know what your mind needs to be at ease, all we have to do is think. We come to the best solutions for ourselves because we literally know everything about ourselves. Tap into this. It's a lot easier than having to explain your everything to someone else who will never understand it the way you do. It's so much more fun to be happy, it's so much easier to be comfortable, just fucking do it.

So far everything in this book has been about the solutions that come with simple thinking. One thing that is not simple at all is the idea of right and wrong. And a more confusing comparison; right and valid.

Right, Logic and Valid

We all have rights. Most of us know what they are, and unfortunately some of us live in places where they're limited. But we understand why they're there; to guarantee human safety and protection. We do have the right to do as we please, go where we want to go, and see who we want to see. Although valid, when we're going through a pandemic it's no longer a matter of rights. I really hope you're not one of those people who believed the government was violating your rights when we were all told to stay at home. From all the surprising things that had happened over the last two years, that whole nonsense was by far one of the most ridiculous.

I tried really hard to make sure everything I said in this book is not cliché. Whenever someone said something regarded as inspirational, or when I read a quote somewhere about these things I always rolled my eyes and thought "not this bullshit". It's like when we look at rules. When we see them as things we're not supposed to do, we try to find ways to break them. But when we see what they actually mean we understand why they're there. The importance is forgetting everything. Forget about everything that is regarded as right or wrong, as good or bad, and just think about it logically. I think that's what they mean when they tell us to do what we believe to be right; making choices without the influence of anything but ourselves.

What's the difference between right and valid? Right is something that is true, purely correct. If you try looking up the definition of valid you'll see it is used widely, even some that come from texting or that wretched application TikTok. This is what became of our world. But validity in terms of knowledge is the consistency of truth. If something is consistent with other ideas, concepts or statements then it is valid.

When we come to conclusions we draw them from our findings. Although things could make sense and are valid, it does not mean that it's right. For example, and this is quite a stupid one but it helps my point; you have skin, oranges also have skin, therefore you're an orange. It's valid, but it's not right. So when it comes to the way of thinking, we calculate the situation and draw up a conclusion from our results. Sometimes, things can make sense but they're not right. The strength is differentiating from right and wrong when it comes to validity.

We all have sins. We all do things that are wrong. When we choose to not do something because we know it's wrong but we want to do it, is that right? If we want something but know it's wrong, doesn't that mean we're currently in a wrong state of mind? Shouldn't we naturally not want something that is wrong for us? Does it matter how we came to the answer? You come to the right answer based on something wrong, but you still get it right. Is that right or is it wrong? Shouldn't it be about what we believe, and not what we think is right?

Most of us have bad habits. We do them knowing they're wrong but it feels right. It makes us feel like we're allowed to be doing them. We get this feeling because we're not hurting anyone by doing it. At the end of the day we're satisfied with what we do and the current path we're on. We even feel like it's something we need to do to stay on track. In a way, what we're doing is valid because it's not interfering with our productivity. Does that make it right? Some might argue that we tell ourselves these things to make us feel better. But even though we tell it to ourselves, it still makes sense.

Since it makes sense, and feels like we're moving ahead in our lives, why shouldn't we think that we're allowed to do certain things during periods of time? If something is wrong but in the general sense everything we're doing is right, does that make it okay?

We're too hard on ourselves when it comes to our faults. And I feel that's one of the best things about humanity. I believe that truly knowing something is wrong is an amazing thing because it shows the kind of people we are. But there are some bad habits that we can't seem to drop, because we feel it's necessary to keep us going at the current period of our lives.

Bad things are regarded as sins because it stops us from doing the good things when we need to. We wouldn't get drunk the moment we wake up because that would ruin the rest of the day. But there's nothing wrong with drinking at night after a long day of work, and it is socially acceptable to go for boozy brunch after a long week. A bad thing is not labelled as a bad thing, it's viewed as a bad thing when it interferes with the good things. It is valid to come to a conclusion where we label things as bad, but don't mention the environment that bad thing manifested in?

Okay, now things are getting confusing. The point is that it's not about what is right and what is wrong. We need to look at it in a way where it's what we believe. If we believe that we're on the right track, and although we have bad habits they don't interfere with what we're doing, then I don't see anything wrong with that. Because ultimately if something *is* bad for us and affects our productivity, we would know. We need to learn to be honest with ourselves, only then will we know what is best for our way of thinking. Time changes, with it so does our perspective.

We discussed before how we each have our own timeline. Everyone does what they're supposed to do when they're supposed to do it. The beginning is the end, and the end is the beginning. This applies to everything we face in life; when we are approaching the end of one stage we are starting a new one. It's a never ending cycle, a cycle that keeps on going till the day we die. We can't really predict how things are going to turn out to be. Predictions are future scenarios made up of expectations, disregarding the idea that we evolve. It's a prediction of how things will be if we maintain our current state of mind. We don't know how our way of thinking will be influenced in the future. We don't even know how it could be influenced tomorrow. Time is like a river, we cannot touch the same water twice because it has already passed, and will never pass again. All we can do is make the most out of the time we have in the current situation.

I want you to do something for me. Everything you have read so far is a descriptive analysis of controlling the way we think and how it affects what we do. I did not try to limit my words but I certainly avoided trying to stretch things out. Everything I have told you are facts when it comes to thinking. I'm not trying to convince you to believe in something I made up; the world is literally that simple and it's our choice whether or not we want to embrace it. What I want you to do is not see anything as being told to you. Actually think about, apply it to a problem you're facing at the moment. Most of the time we're told things and we do them because we believe we should. That's not right, because we have to believe in what we live by. Do you believe the world is simple? Do you believe that we're misinformed and manipulated to believe that it's something a lot more complicated?

We spoke about how racism is an idea that should be eliminated from our world. For us to do that we need to understand where it came from. People are taught certain things about certain cultures. Many American towns have been taught to believe that all Arabs are terrorists who spend their days on camels or blowing themselves up. How did they come to this conclusion? If someone is taught something when they're growing up and go on to believe it, isn't that a valid way of thinking? Someone told you something, you see the evidence, and although sometimes the evidence can be either wrong or tampered with they come to their conclusion. We mentioned before how the United States has no history. What they're taught in 'American History' is how they were so heroic during the world wars, and how nuking Hiroshima was a necessary act. What's interesting is that even those who teach don't find the importance of opening the minds of their youth to the reality of the world. That is wrong.

I spoke a little bit about America, not in the best way. I just want to make it clear that I have a lot of American friends who are cultured and open-minded. It's not just the United States that are guilty of closed-mindedness, there are others as well. Every society has opposing thoughts, because every person tries to live a valid life. It is *normal* and *encouraged* for people to be different. Cancel culture does not solve the problem, but understanding someone's validity and having the logic and space to understand (or ignore!) might.

Neo-Nazism is still a thing in Germany, especially in their underworld. They refer to those with Turkish origins as trash who don't deserve to be in their country. Who taught them this? The people who came before them. Their way of thinking is valid because that is what they were taught, and that is what was shown to them as they grew up. If you can't see through the lies, then you don't know enough about the issue. And that's the problem with our world; people are taught the wrong things at an early age and it becomes their way of thinking. We can't really blame them because it originated from the older generations who passed it down. They are taught these things through the meaning of collective memory and false loyalty, and pass it down with shame and hatred.

Imagine an island populated with one thousand people, and another next to it also populated with one thousand people. The first island declares war for unreasonable causes, and attacks. The armies fight against each other and the first island wins. They slaughter the entire enemy flank, and win the war. With that victory they now have the power to make things seem the way they want. No one is going to stop them, do you really think they're going to admit their wrongs? History is written by the victors, we know this.

If Hitler won the Second World War, would the fact that he burnt millions of Jews be talked about? When you read about the world wars you'll notice that the United Kingdom and those who fought beside them are referred to as the allies. They're literally calling themselves the good guys. It's not the question of whether or not history is real, it's to what extent are the ones who win telling the truth, and how much are they hiding.

History is all recorded, and it builds up to where we are now, making it valid. But to what extent is it right? Who controls what is said when we are taught history. If Japan had been one of the victors of World War II, how would the state of the world be now?

I feel I said a little too much about the United States, and I don't want to be stopped at customs the next time I'm craving Minetta's Tavern in New York. So I'm going to leave you with this on the subject; why should we believe what governments tell us happened when the ones who won are the ones that wrote down history?

You're sitting in a pub and it's pretty crowded. You know two identical twins named Balthazar and Nebecednazer. You're a lot closer to Nebecednazer than you are to Balthazar. So when Balthazar walks into the pub you think it's Nebecednazer, and you tell yourself "oh shit Neb is here". Nebecednazer is actually there, he's just on one of the tables behind you and you haven't seen him yet. You came to the conclusion that he's here when you saw his brother, who you thought was him. He actually was in the pub, but you came to that conclusion based on wrong evidence. Is that true knowledge?

Ethics is something we all like to believe we have. We mentioned Hitler, if you'd go back in time (even though we distinguished that you can't) and you see Hitler as a baby in front of you, would you kill him? Of course not. Why is it even something to consider? It's a fucking baby, I don't care if it's Satan. A better scenario to judge someone's ethics is the bus driver one. You're a bus driver, and in the bus you have fifty children below the age of fifteen. You're driving right by a cliff and all of a sudden one of your family members is just standing there in the middle of the road. Your only choices are to either run over that family member of yours, and drive off the cliff killing you and fifty children. I'm not going to lie to you, I'll drive off the cliff without a second thought. One of the many reasons I won't become a bus driver. The interesting thing about this scenario is that both choices have right and wrong in them. It's just that one of them involves you killing fifty people over just one person. But that person is someone you love. Shouldn't that come into play? Why should it be a matter of numbers rather than a matter of who the people are. Of course, the children are all important to someone. But you're the one driving the bus, not one of their parents. You make the choice. We all like to believe we would make the ethical choice; we run over our family members to save all the children. The truth is no one knows exactly what they would do in that situation.

It's all about making choices, and for us to trust ourselves in certain situations we need to respect the way we think. Everything you have read sounds simple, and trust me it's not that complex to actually do. You'll find yourself being misunderstood a lot, and that just shows you have so much more to you than what people see. It is better to be misunderstood for doing something you want and truly believe in than being understood for complying to fucked up societal norms.

Those of us who have lost someone we care about know that it is one of the hardest things we go through in life. Sadness is the primary emotion during those times, and nothing can help but time. The hardest part about it is that we feel no one else understands what we're going through. We feel no one else knows the relationship we had with that person; the level of love and admiration. It's what we all feel when we lose someone we love. It is the essence of grief.

Most of us believe that there is an afterlife, and we know the basic idea; if we're good we go to heaven, and if we're bad we go to hell. Hopefully from now on we're more motivated to do good so we don't spend eternity burning in the fires of hell.

The one thing every single religion or culture has is their own idea of an afterlife. It's one of the few things in this world we know absolutely nothing about when it comes to facts. It's not a surprise that it's one of the things in common because people need an idea for what is to come, otherwise the fear of not knowing will take over.

I don't know what you believe in exactly when it comes to the idea of afterlife, but I'm going to discuss it in the context of heaven and hell, as it is what I believe.

We live in a world filled with experiences to test us, and some of these tests can be cruel. One of the toughest things to face is losing someone. The sad part is the idea that we're never seeing them again during our time in this world, which hopefully for all of us will be a very long time after living a positive, prosperous, wholesome life. But when we actually think of it, our time on Earth is barely a fraction of our existence. It's scary to think what comes next; wondering what exactly is waiting for us and how it never ends. But why trouble ourselves with stage two when there's still so much to do in stage one?

It's interesting to realize that all you have to do is make the right choices and you're put into paradise forever. Think about it as though it's an actual test you would take in school. Some questions are easy; they don't require much thinking for you to answer it right. Some questions are hard. And just because it's hard doesn't mean you stress out and fill in the wrong answer. There's nothing wrong with taking the time to do extra thinking for certain problems.

Up until now we talked about the multiple approaches to the situations we face. We saw that the most logical approaches in life are in fact the right ones. We sometimes think doing the wrong thing is easier, but putting in the wrong answer in a test just because we don't want to think a little bit longer is still the wrong answer. It's that simple in a school test and it's that simple in life. We are so capable of overthinking that the simplicity of situations is never really seen.

Again, I am going to keep saying this so you don't misunderstand; I don't believe I have the best methods of thinking, but it definitely helped me. It's not something I convince myself to think; it's logical, it makes sense, and it's true.

People die younger than others, people die in worse ways than others, and people die when their time is done and they're ready to go to a better place. In the end, people die at their time because death is the only thing we can be sure of in this life. It's important to remember that this is not like one of those rules I mentioned earlier; something to just believe. It's true, understand it and accept it, why wouldn't you want to? Fear?

When someone we love dies, all we have left is the effect they had on us from the time they were with us. When we're told that the people we love may be dead, but are not gone, they mean that a person's existence isn't just being there. Even when we're alive, just being there isn't what matters to people; it's how we make them feel. The next time we see the people we lost we will never lose them again. So until then, what they left us with is enough to keep us going because they didn't choose to leave us. No one wants to see the people they care about hurt, and if God forbid any of us were to suddenly die we know we wouldn't want them to fall apart.

Death in this world brings life in heaven. That's enough to know that just because someone dies doesn't mean they seize to exist. They did their part, it's a reminder for us to do ours so that when the time comes we are proud of the life we led. The feeling of emptiness is difficult to avoid, and it shouldn't be fought. It's not exactly emptiness, it's just that the person was such a huge part of us that the pain is a lot to bear.

What's interesting with that sense is that we feel things are falling apart, and the heartbreak is too big to be healed. Grief is a wound. The pain we feel is because of the enormous amount of love we feel towards that person, that *one* person. That should make us realize that our hearts are a lot bigger than they seem, and we're all capable of feeling to an infinite extent.

If you've lost a mother or a father, continue doing what you were doing when they were alive and proud of you, but from then you'll be living with their eternal influence celebrating their lives with every choice you make. They were proud of you for what you did in the first part of your life, imagine how proud they're going to be when you continue doing better in the next. No one wants to see their children live a miserable life without them, so let them see that they did their part. Allow them to be successful in what they were meant to do; always guide you to the right choice even when they're not there to tell you themselves.

People die young, and the saddest part is that they had their whole lives ahead of them. We can't really say that, can we? There is no 'what if' in this world. Everything that is supposed to happen, happens. Death is a right. I have lost a few friends over the years, and they were amazing people. I once asked myself why people die so young when they've done nothing to deserve it. But then you remember that no one deserves to die. Whether old or young, when a person's time comes, it comes. Death is a right.

If you've lost a son or a daughter no one can begin to imagine your pain. It is always said that a parent should never have to outlive their children. We can't assume this world is cruel when it comes to nature. There is already so much cruelty that is brought by people, we must believe that everything happens for a reason. You must know that your child was so extraordinary that they were too good for the world. They were called up to become angels and watch over you, rather than you watch over them. We don't know exactly what happens when people die, but wouldn't you rather believe in something beautiful that is more likely to be true?

Albus Dumbledore told us to pity the living and not the dead. That was to convey how we see the afterlife as something so dark when in truth it's the world that's dark. But I don't believe that either. I don't think we should pity anyone, because everyone is on their own timeline. The dead have done their time, we're still in ours. It's important to not let it affect the way we continue to live our lives.

The idea of losing ourselves benefits no one. Not ourselves, not the people around us, not even the people we've lost. It's easy to break down, and it's okay for it to happen when it happens, because the pain can be too much. But the importance is getting back up. Those who look over us expect us to excel, not to break down. It's logical; we should continue to make them proud, just because they're not there anymore doesn't mean they can't see us, and it doesn't mean their love for us is gone.

Like I mentioned, when a person dies their physical presence is what's gone. Look at the people around you who you're close to, can you see their love? Can you physically see their effects on you? It's difficult to feel these things when they're gone but they're always there. We are made up of the love and experiences handed to us, and we grieve those sources when they leave us.

I always wondered what they meant when they say the people we lose will always be in our heart. We talked a lot about emotion but not once did I define it; it's a strong feeling coming from our circumstances or our relationships with others. Our emotions are not just feelings, they're connections. The connections we have to the people and world around us. With what we feel the people we have lost continue to live on. This is not something to tell yourself so you feel better, it's true. None of us will live forever, but the positive impact we have on others carries on, sometimes past the person you impacted. It passes to their loved ones, their coworkers, etc. By building a positive attitude you commit to a positive network, which manifests as a positive source of energy for your societies, and then can carry on to other societies. Small ripples, enough to make waves in the ocean of time.

What else is this feeling we get when it comes to the people we care about? Why do we feel such pain when someone we love passes? When something happens to someone we care about we feel pain. No matter what it is, when people we care about get hurt, so do we. It's as simple as one of our loved ones feeling upset. We feel their pain and it affects us. So it's no surprise that when someone dies we feel unbearable pain and grief. What's important is that even though something happened to them, they're not gone. We are greater than the sum of our parts, they were more than just the body they inhabited. Their love lingers. Their love transcends. Their love survives, and it is our duty to carry it on.

    Many people have lost a lot of loved ones in the last year. The coronavirus spread quickly and took a lot of lives. The problem with that virus is that it has so many symptoms and affects a lot of different parts of the body, which makes it so deadly and *random*. Some are more susceptible due to previous medical conditions and are more vulnerable to some of the symptoms. Whether the conspiracy of this whole pandemic being exploited is true or not is unknown, and honestly I don't care. We've seen the way people have responded in the last year. Disregarding those idiots who thought their rights were being breached, the majority of the world showed unification when it came to the support of those affected and those in the medical profession risking their lives everyday. There was a global shift. The virus was a reminder of how fragile life is. Think properly, think clearly, and think logically. Think calmly, survey the situation, and surrender to it. There is so much bullshit in this world, to the point where it really influences the way we think. We need to remember to take all of that out because what we have inside of us is more than enough to keep ourselves going. The continued increase in logic with every situation we face allows us to move forward to the next situation with something to gain. The people we care about – especially the ones we've lost – are what make us feel certain emotions and emphasize the ones we choose to hold on to. There's so much good in this world, we should live to do good so that we reap all the benefits of this level before we go on to the next. We need to remember to believe, because the idea of losing faith has become extremely old and lame. Species die out when they keep repeating the same mistakes; we should face the inevitable and do something. We all know we're going to die. We all know our time here is barely a fraction of our existence. Dumbledore also said "to the well organized mind, death is but the next great adventure".

It's like tiring yourself studying for an exam so that when you pass you relax with satisfaction. Let's learn to think a bit longer and harder so that we pass every test we face. When death comes we welcome it knowing we did our part. I hope we all live long lives that are filled with the choices made by us, not by influence. Once we learn to think logically and choose our actions then we've found the true meaning of happiness.

There are so many beliefs when it comes to death, I like to follow the logical one. The one that gives me hope rather than despair. Have you ever played solitaire? If you have, you'd remember then when you're about to finish a level they automatically do it for you. You see all the cards go where they need to go. Besides the fact that it's satisfying to watch, it's interesting to think that that's how life is. Everything is happening the way it's supposed to, and from up there it's a lot faster than it feels down here. We really need to live life believing that everything is coming to us as fast as it could, and although our paths are determined, let's ensure it's a great one by thinking logically with every situation we face. At the same time consider what is right and what is wrong.

We're all capable of it, it just requires a little bit of extra thinking, but we all have time for that if we let go of the immediate satisfaction guarantee we have become addicted to. I hope I was successful in making things sound simple. I believe that complexity comes when people try to be smart and make things sound like it's more than what it is. True intelligence is recognizing when something doesn't require a lot of unnecessary effort, but a good amount of logical approaches.

www.ingramcontent.com/pod-product-compliance
Lightning Source LLC
Chambersburg PA
CBHW070740230426
43669CB00014B/2524